BLACK ROBIN
COUNTRY

To Sally

BLACK ROBIN COUNTRY

The Chatham Islands and its Wildlife

by

David Cemmick

Text by Dick Veitch

HODDER AND STOUGHTON
AUCKLAND   LONDON   SYDNEY   TORONTO

Copyright © 1985 David Cemmick and Dick Veitch
First published 1985
ISBN 0 340 358262

All rights reserved. No part of this publication may be reproduced or transmitted in any form or by any means, electronic or mechanical including photocopy, recording, or any information storage and retrieval system, without permission in writing from the publisher.

Typeset by Saba Graphics Ltd, Christchurch.
Printed and bound in Hong Kong for Hodder & Stoughton Ltd,
44-46 View Road, Glenfield, Auckland, New Zealand.

Contents

Foreword	7
Author's Note	9
Acknowledgements	11
Introduction	13
The Chathams	15
The Team	26
South East Island	33
The Fostering Project	64
The Foster Parents	70
Mangere Island	95
A Growing Population	112
The Next Year, the Year After...	132
Appendix: Chatham Island Birds	134

BLACK ROBIN

Foreword

THE WHOLE WORLD should read this book, and hold its breath, in hope.

This is a natural history in the classic sense of the word: an account by two dedicated people, one a conservationist, the other an artist, who were drawn together by a love and respect for wildlife, wild places, and, above all, wild birds, to record for posterity the natural wonders of Black Robin Country.

But it is much more than that. It is a story of hope in a microcosm of this sad twentieth century world, the people of which seem hell bent on destroying their natural heritage, and with it themselves.

Black Robin Country is, or rather was, the Chathams, a group of some fourteen plus islands, 870 kilometres east of Christchurch, New Zealand. When first settled by the Moriori some 1100 years ago, it was a natural paradise of forest and windswept peatlands, the home of a wealth of insects and birds. It was discovered by Europeans in 1791, and was settled some thirty-five years later.

Since the first people arrived on this small group of islands, more than thirty sorts of birds have joined the much more famous dodo among the ranks of the extinct. Of the present forty-three native species, no fewer than twelve subspecies and five species are endemic, which means they can be found nowhere else on earth. Most of these are today rare, and the rarest is *Petroica traversi*, the black robin, which holds the distinction of being the rarest bird in the world.

These tragic losses and this sad state of affairs are due to hunting, habitat destruction for farming, and the introduction of exotic animals. As with mainland New Zealand, the Chathams were devoid of terrestrial mammals until people came on the scene.

Apart from man himself, the mammals introduced were rats, cats, pigs, goats, sheep and cattle. The result of their destructive presence was the retreat of the native plants and animals to ever smaller refugia on the smallest islands. Two of these are the Mangeres, Big and Little.

So it was that in 1900 all the black robins which then remained in the world were to be found, with great difficulty, in one hectare (a mere 10,000 square metres) of degenerating forest on Little Mangere. Seventy-six years later the total population was known to be two females and five males, one of the females being at least six years of age. Something had to be done, and done immediately, or this delightful bird would become just another memory.

Black Robin Country takes up the story from here. It is a fascinating history of the relocation of the dwindling robin population, of brief success, and of disappointment; a story of experiment with foster parents and model eggs, and of hair-raising journeys, transporting makeshift incubators in small boats. But the outcome is still unknown. The work continues and the future of the world's rarest bird still hangs in delicate balance. New Zealand holds her breath in hope.

New Zealand is one of the most beautiful countries on earth, a beauty made up of a diversity of landscapes, each clothed with unique vegetation upon which depends a rich fauna, many members of which are also unique. In its natural heritage it is one of the richest countries in the world; unfortunately, in terms of modern economics, its GNP leaves much to be desired. It is thus very easy for some to say, 'Why spend money on trying to save the black robin, kauri pine, takahe, kiwi etc. Profits are more important. Down with native plants and animals; more sheep, more *Pinus radiata*, more profit. That's what provides jobs.'

Fortunately there is a growing band of people who vote not only with their ballot papers but with their voices, time, expertise and money, to promote pride in a unique heritage which, if conserved, will repay both them and their children's children 10,000-fold. As well as providing a diverse and beautiful environment in which to live, it will attract an ever larger tourist trade, and jobs for the future.

Petroica traversi is a living symbol of that pride, and of the conservation movement. If this small bird becomes extinct it will indeed be a black day. And so the world waits with baited breath...

David Bellamy
Bedburn, 1985

Geranium chathamica

Author's Note

I DID NOT actually meet David Cemmick until he arrived at Auckland's Mangere Airport in September 1983. The events leading up to this book, however, began long before that.

During a visit to Great Britain in 1982, I saw in a friend's house there, a handsome watercolour of a Scottish wild cat trying to catch a ptarmigan. My host informed me that the artist, David Cemmick, lived nearby and suggested we meet. But it was not until after my return to New Zealand that we made acquaintance — by letter.

In photographs of David's paintings I saw an artist with a genuine recognition of, and ability to portray, the proportions, shape and form of wild animals. With an interesting work programme planned for the 1983 spring — including a long visit to the Chatham Islands — I invited David to join me, having little thought of the possibility of this book. The prime reason for me, as an officer of the Wildlife Service, in visiting the Chatham Islands, was to continue the work of helping the very rare black robin to survive — a project that had been started in 1976. I know now that for David this trip was a once-in-a-lifetime chance that he had been determined not to miss.

Soon after his arrival David joined a Royal Australasian Ornithologists Union visit to Little Barrier Island. He then visited Great Barrier Island, home of the rare brown teal, and the Bay of Plenty and Coromandel to paint landscapes of places visited by Captain Cook.

Following this part of his visit, we teamed up to travel south — to see the sights, visit friends and get our mountain of Chatham Islands equipment as far as Wellington. En route there were many places to explore: Otorohanga, with its fine kiwi house and huge walk-through aviary; the trout hatchery at Turangi; predator-free Kapiti Island with its prolific bird life; the relatively silent forests of the Akatarawa Valley; and Mount Bruce Native Bird Reserve where common, not so common, and some very rare birds are being bred for release into repaired natural habitats or for education and research.

So David met New Zealanders, saw some of the top half of the country, some forest, some birds and some conservation problems, and we both got safely to Wellington in readiness for the Chatham Islands expedition.

For many years staff of the New Zealand Wildlife Service, Department of Internal Affairs, with permission from the owners, have been visiting the smaller islands of the Chatham group. Sheep have been removed from islands, huts built, trees planted, eggs and birds moved from island to island, and eggs swapped from nest to nest — all in a bid to save the black robin from extinction.

Black Robin Country is the story of a desperate rescue mission. It is also an informal record of one particular expedition in the summer of 1983 to South East and Little Mangere islands, telling of the places where we stayed, the bird life, and the fascinating things we saw. Little did we expect that this would be the wettest summer since 1946, and such a good breeding season for the black robins, so much so that their numbers would more than double.

Dick Veitch
Auckland, 1985

Chatham Island Petrel — Pterodroma hypoleuca axillaris.

Acknowledgements

MANY PEOPLE HAVE assisted us in many ways in the preparation of this book. We are grateful to them all.

Mr and Mrs S. Still instigated David Cemmick's visit to New Zealand, and were the first to help with his financial needs. Further assistance was given by the Peter Nathan Cultural Trust, Windsor and Newton (in the form of art materials supplied), the Augustine Trust, the Pamela Sheridan Trust, and the Darlington Borough Council.

Financial sponsorship and support came also from: Mr and Mrs C. Cemmick, Mr and Mrs G. Cole, Mr and Mrs C. Denton, Mr, Mrs and John Duell, Mr and Mrs G.W. Forbes, Mrs J. Gardner, Mr and Mrs M. Grace, Mrs P. Nichol, Mr and Mrs P. Richardson, Mr P. Robinson of Thomas Watson & Sons, Mr and Mrs R. Sellars, Mr and Mrs C. Smith, Mr and Mrs P. Smyth, Mr and Mrs Taylor, Mr C. Walker, Mr A. Wilkinson, and Mr J. Wood.

Written personal references supporting David Cemmick were given by: Mr Ian Armstrong of the Royal Society for the Protection of Birds, Dr David Bellamy, Mr Michael Clegg, and Miss Julie Gaman of the Durham County Conservation Trust.

The director and senior staff of the New Zealand Wildlife Service granted permission and made arrangements for this visit to the Chatham Islands. In the field we received able assistance from Don Merton, Nigel Miller, Allan Munn and Geordie Murman, and during our brief time on the main Chatham Island we appreciated the hospitality of David and Jan Jenner.

Mr Stuart Park and Dr Brian Gill of the Auckland Institute and Museum, Mr Phil Millener of the National Museum, and Mr Russell Thomas assisted with visual references for the few birds we could not see in the wild. We thank also Brian Bell, David Crockett, Geoff Kelly, Don Merton, and Doug Sutton for the information they have supplied.

During preparation of the manuscript we received excellent help and advice from Paul Cemmick and Geoff Halpin (graphics and cover layout), and David Canning, Don Merton and Rod Morris.

Special thanks is due to Mr and Mrs C. Cemmick for their general help and support.

Last, but far from least, we recognise and greatly appreciate the unstinting efforts of the ladies who stayed at home — Elizabeth and Bryony.

Introduction

THE BLACK ROBIN, *Petroica (Miro) traversi*, must surely have existed on all the larger islands of the Chatham group, but by the time the first ornithological records were compiled in 1871, it was found only on Mangere and Little Mangere islands. Within the next 30 years cats were introduced to Mangere and the robins were all eaten. That left the total world population of black robins in one hectare of forest on the top of Little Mangere Island.

During visits to the island in 1937, 1961 and 1968, ornithologists estimated the robin population to vary from 13 to 35 pairs. In the early 1970s a study was begun; all the birds were colour banded and, by October 1973, the black robin population was known to be only six pairs and four extra males.

At about this time the one hectare forest on Little Mangere began to degenerate — partly owing to a series of very dry years, and partly owing to the clearing of an area of forest for a helicopter landing place to facilitate the illegal taking of muttonbirds. This allowed salt-laden winds to enter the forest and kill trees which would normally be protected by the hardy coastal belt.

By September 1976 there were only seven black robins left: two females and five males. For these few to survive, a new home was needed.

In 1966 the Royal Forest and Bird Protection Society of New Zealand had joined forces with the Government and purchased Mangere Island for management as a nature reserve. A decade of hard work saw the removal of the introduced animals, and the replanting and rehabilitation of the native forest which was showing good signs of regeneration.

So the whole world population of black robins was transferred to the relative safety of the regenerating forest. It was a desperate move, but it worked, for the robins settled down in their new island home, and, what is more important, began to breed; even the old female took part. Unfortunately it was not enough. The robin's natural rate of reproduction was far too slow. Although capable of laying many eggs, the robin can rear only one or two young each year. Something more drastic had to be done.

It became clear that, if the black robin was to survive, it would need the help of foster parents to raise its young. After much experimentation with various birds, Don Merton found that the Chatham Island tit, *Petroica macrocephala chathamensis*, a close relative of the black robin which is not on Mangere Island but is reasonably abundant on South East Island, was the only totally successful foster parent.

While the black robin rescue story began on Mangere Island, the focus of the Wildlife Service's attention has more recently been on South East Island, with all efforts being made to increase the robin population by using the tit foster parents. It was to help in this fostering work, which had been in progress since 1980, that we made the trip to the Chathams.

Cuba Channel
Air Strip
Te Whanga Lagoon
Hanson Bay
Petré Bay
Chatham Island
Waitangi
Owenga
Taiko Camp
Pitt Strait
Sentry Reef
CHATHAM ISLANDS
Mangere Island
Pitt Island
(Rangiauria)
Sail Rock
South East Island
(Rangatira)
Round Rock
South Reef
Fancy Rock
The Pyramid
N

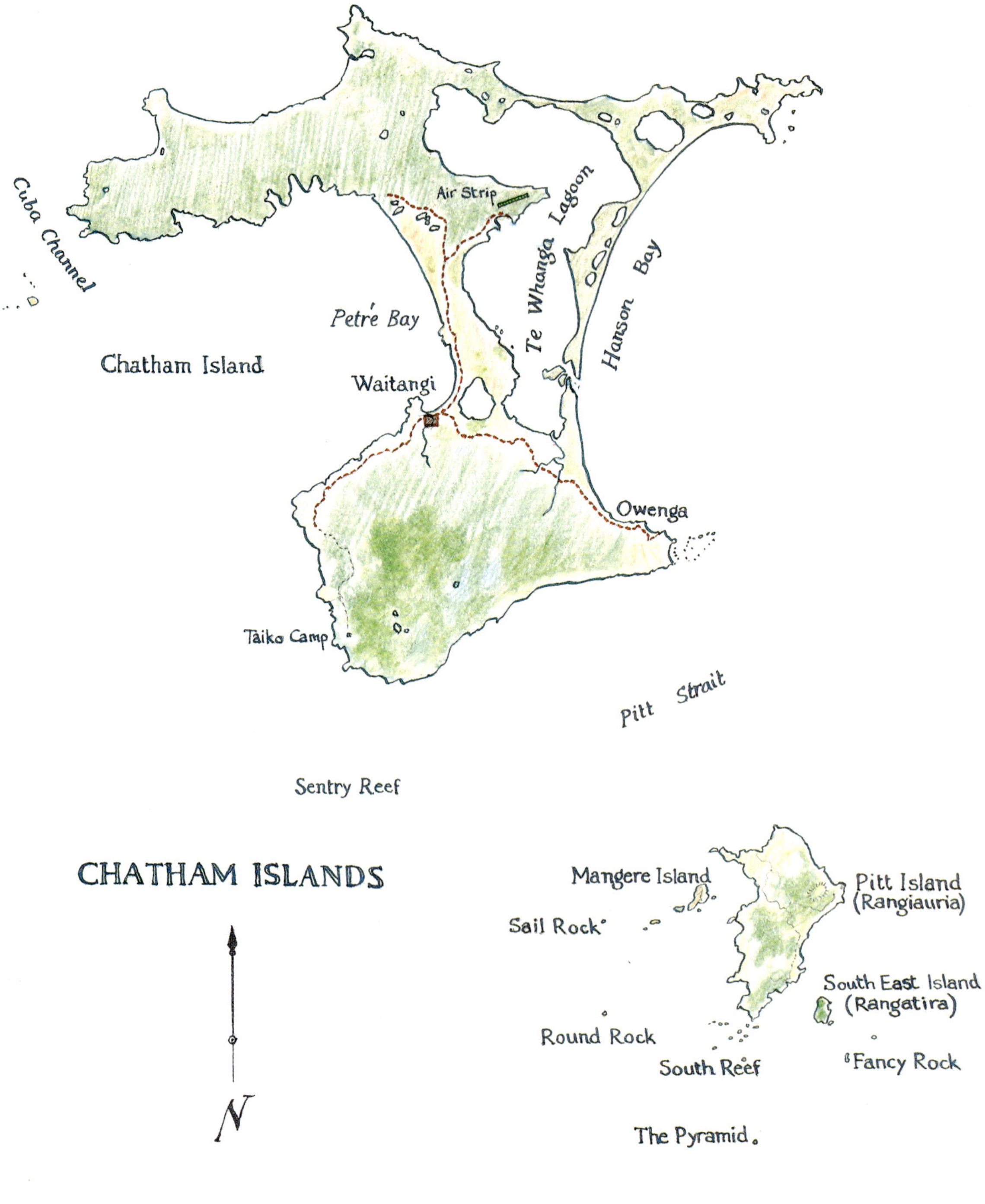

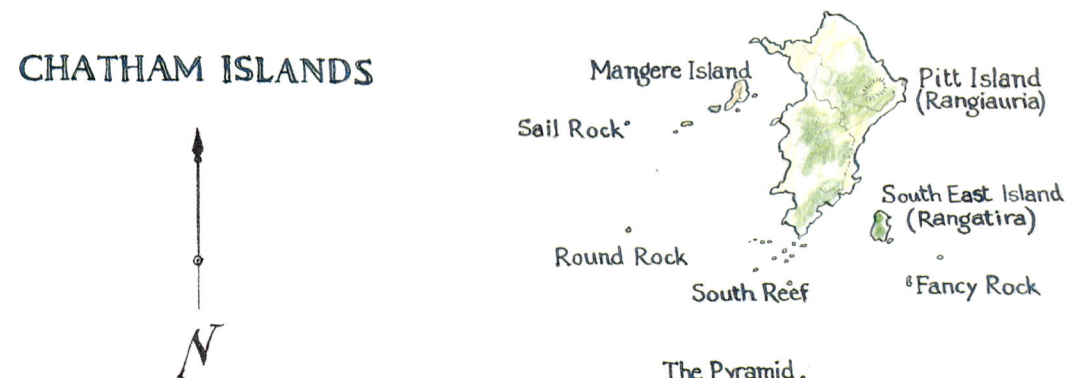

The Chathams

GETTING TO THE Chathams is not the adventure it once was. The only means of transport used to be by ship. My first trip was four hours in the 'comfort' of a Bristol Freighter. Today the four-engined Argosy, with room for 30 passengers, is there in just two or three hours, depending on the wind. We dropped out of the clouds too late to see the large southern end of the main Chatham Island. The first impression instead was of lagoons, narrow bits of land, bracken, grass and sheep in almost equal proportions, with a scattering of golden-flowered gorse in between.

Mainland New Zealanders either know a little about the Chathams, think of them as an idyllic spot 'somewhere out there', or hear about them only at the end of the weather forecast when rain and wind is usually predicted.

The Chatham Islands comprise an archipelago of two large and more than a dozen smaller islands and rocks about latitude 44° south and longitude 176° 30′ west, placing them about 870 kilometres east of Christchurch. The climate is moderate, with temperatures varying little from an average of 11 degrees Celsius. The annual rainfall average is about 850 millimetres.

The group is of volcanic origin. The main island of 90,000 hectares now appears as a series of low hills joined by wide vegetated sandbars creating a large central brackish water lagoon of some 16,000 hectares and a number of smaller lagoons, with significant blocks of land to the south and northwest. The lack of slope, combined with the local climate, has resulted in the formation of large areas of peatland.

The highest point on the main island is just 293 metres above sea level. The other large islands in the group are: Pitt Island, with 6203 hectares, no higher but more undulating in nature; South East Island with 218 hectares, rising to 224 metres; and Mangere Island with 113 hectares, rising to 287 metres, and both have a sloping terrain.

For tens of thousands of years much of the Chathams was covered in forest: not the tall forest we know from the mainland but a considerably lower one with many different tree species. In and about this forest lived many birds which were found only on the Chathams. No land mammals were present. Today most of these forests have gone and those that remain have been heavily modified by man and his four-footed camp followers.

The first known people to come to these islands, about 1100 years ago, were the Moriori. There are many myths, legends and stories about their origin, arrival and lifestyle. Clearly though, they travelled from New Zealand to these islands. They were a people not inclined to fight; they had no dogs with them (as the Maori had in New Zealand); and they did not cultivate the land. A rat, the kiore, did accompany the first settlers, and it is likely that their fires accidentally destroyed some forest.

Moriori life seems to have centred about the seal colonies — a major food source — where the new inhabitants built permanent dwellings and shelters. Other food was obtained during irregular or seasonal visits to shellfish beds and bird colonies to gather whatever could be found or for the seasonal crop of chicks. Despite the absence of large trees for canoes, the Moriori constructed craft by bundling together smaller timbers and so were able to travel to almost all the islands of the group.

Today, to the casual observer, there is no sign of the early Moriori presence. But indications do exist, such as the dendroglyphs (tree carvings) and petroglyphs (rock carvings) which depict important aspects of Moriori life (*see opposite*).

European discovery of the Chathams on 29 November 1791 was a quite accidental event, when HMS *Chatham*, under the command of Lieutenant William R. Broughton, was blown off course en route from England to Tahiti.

Seal hunting by Europeans began about ten years later. At that time there were reports that in many places the island was on fire. Many gangs of sealers lived on the main islands for long periods. With them they brought disease, and they looked upon the more than 2000 Moriori present at that time as little more than beasts. By 1830 the seal population was almost destroyed, but at least one ship is reported to have completed its cargo with timber, pork, potatoes and flax — goods presumably grown or gathered by sealers who are recorded as first living permanently on Chatham Island as early as 1827.

By this time whaling had become an important industry with ships coming from Australia, England, France, North America, Peru and Portugal. Onshore whaling bases were also established. When the industry reached its peak in 1840 more than 20 ships were regularly present, but by 1870 only one vessel was working the area.

Late in 1835 some 900 Maori of the Ngati Mutunga and Ngati Tama tribes, who had left Taranaki with Te Rauparaha, decided they would benefit by migrating to the Chathams. The number of Moriori present at this time was probably low owing to the virtual absence of seals. The population was further reduced by the Maori who enslaved and, occasionally, massacred and ate them. The Maori also fought among themselves and by 1861 there were only some 413 Maori on the islands. The Moriori population at this time numbered 160, and the European, 46.

Moriori petroglyphs or rock carvings, interpreted as seals (*above*) and penguins (*below*).

It is recorded, however, that by this time sufficient land was being cultivated for 1000 tons of wheat and potatoes to be exported in one year — a far cry from the uncultivated land of 1800.

While the early sealers did report peat fires burning, there is no certainty about the extent of the original natural forest, or how much it was modified by the Moriori. We do know that there are now fewer than 8000 hectares of forest left on the main Chatham Island — just 11 per cent of the land area. Some patches of this forest are too small and others too modified to be satisfactory wildlife habitats. Fortunately, some of the more far-sighted landowners have fenced, or gifted to the Crown as reserves, a few large areas so that examples of Chatham Island forest will be preserved.

Unfortunately, as everywhere else, the arrival of Europeans was accompanied by the introduction of a number of animals which, for the native wildlife and forests, were a threat. Pigs were reported as being plentiful by 1831, and European rats and mice had plenty of opportunity to get ashore by then. Cats probably did not live in the wild until after the first European families arrived in the 1840s. Since then hedgehogs and possums have been introduced. By good fortune in the early years, and good management more recently, only cats, mice, wekas and pigs have reached Pitt Island. Today there are also wild sheep and cattle in all unfenced forest areas.

Thus, forest destruction, the introduction of animals, and possibly hunting by man, have caused the complete or near extinction of a number of birds on the Chathams.

Archaeological evidence from material dating back to about the year 1500 suggests that at that time the Moriori found, and apparently ate, a large variety of birds. Some of these, such as the crested penguin, mottled petrel, grey teal, and scaup, were present in numbers large enough to indicate that they bred on the Chatham Islands. None of these species are there now, but they are still found in other parts of New Zealand. Of greater interest are the now extinct Chatham Island goose duck, a merganser, a giant rail and a snipe, which was distinctly larger than the snipe still found there. Curiously, the petrel and duck bones found, amongst material dating back to 1500, reveal species different from any other found in the world today. Also recorded, but without such accurate knowledge on their period of existence, are the New Zealand swan, coot, Chatham Island fish eagle, and weka (reintroduced 1905).

After Europeans arrived, the brown teal, falcon, shoveler and paradise ducks disappeared, as did the fernbird, bellbird, and two endemic Chatham Island species of rail. The rail and fernbird were almost surely eradicated by the combined effects of rats and cats. The other birds were lost when man destroyed an important part of their habitat.

Life for the people on the Chatham Islands is very different from that of most mainlanders. A plane, with room for 30 passengers and perishable freight, goes from Wellington or Christchurch once or twice a week. For heavier goods there is a ship every four or five weeks. The economy of the islands revolves around farming and fishing. About one third of the human

Chatham Island forget-me-not.

population of 560 is part of, or related to, the public service activities of Post Office, communications, law enforcement, County Council and hospital. To make life 'civilised' there is one store, one garage, one hotel and one policeman. The farmers have difficulties with transportation, as well as other problems typical of small communities remote from sources of supply. Fishing still focuses on the delicious crayfish.

Today the two main islands of Chatham and Pitt continue to be modified by man. They have their reserves and they still have their introduced animals. By good fortune, however, no cats, rats, mice, hedgehogs, pigs or possums are on Mangere or South East islands. So it is to these places that we go in our attempts to save some of the world's rarest birds. Foremost among these is the Chatham Island black robin whose total population in 1980 had further declined to just two females and three males. Our work and travels on this occasion took us first to South East Island and then, briefly, to Mangere Island.

Chatham Island Taiko *Pterodroma magentae*
Many islands have an almost exclusive abundance of one species of petrel. The main Chatham island, and possibly Pitt Island, had the taiko. The young of this species appear to have been exploited by the Moriori as a muttonbird, but this should not have been unduly detrimental to the overall population. The taiko disappeared soon after the arrival of European man, presumably as a result of the introduction of cats and rats and the burning of the forests. Only one specimen, collected in the middle of last century, exists in a museum, and ornithological literature early this century ignored the species' existence. However, in recent years, the curiosity of wildlife enthusiast David Crockett has been aroused and, on an entirely voluntary basis, he has led twelve expeditions, involving 107 people in all, to the Chathams to locate the taiko. So far, some 45 birds have been seen and 23 caught and banded. Five of these have been caught a second time, with one bird having a muddy bill and breast. No breeding place has been found, however.

The drawings here are from photographs taken by another enthusiast, Russell Thomas.

'TAIKO'

Buff Weka *Gallirallus australis hectori*
Undated archaeological evidence shows quite clearly that a weka very like this species was on the main Chatham island at some time in the past, but in an archaeological dig on the island no weka bones were found among Moriori artifacts with a known age of about the year 1500. If wekas were still there then, and as easy to catch as the present bird, it is curious that the Moriori did not eat them. Some early European writings suggest that they were present until 1868, but there may have been some confusion over the use of the name 'weka', for one early photograph of a banded rail is labelled 'weka'. Certainly, wekas were not present in 1905 when new stock was reintroduced from Canterbury, where they are now extinct. On the main Chatham and Pitt islands they are now so numerous that Chatham Islanders are allowed to hunt them for food.

Weka after a bath!

♀ feeding chick on worm.
note 'bobbed' tail as adult.

Wind blowing up a frill of feathers

Weka feeding on cow-pasture near Waitangi — four chicks fed by both parent birds on mainly worms. They were very confiding and came within three feet of me whilst I sketched.

Dark red eye - cream lids.
Amber/brick large leg scales.

Inquisitive, wild direct look - typically rail!

characteristic 'cocked' tail.

'DON'

The Team

THE TEAM FOR our trip comprised six people, and supplies entailed equipment and three months' provisions. Like almost all previous expeditions to these islands, this visit was organised by the New Zealand Wildlife Service, with the main objective being the further management of the black robin.

Leader of the team was Don Merton: a man with an all-consuming interest in birds. For some years he has been Principal Wildlife Officer (Endangered Species) and therefore responsible for the rarest of our rare birds, particularly the kakapo (a large, flightless, polygamous and nocturnal parrot), and the black robin. He also has close contact with the very difficult projects to save the takahe (another flightless bird) and black stilt, and has a watching brief over the other 28 endangered bird species throughout New Zealand. Planning for the actual management work keeps him busy so, for this expedition, the organising of food and camp equipment was delegated to 'Nog' — more correctly known as Allan Munn.

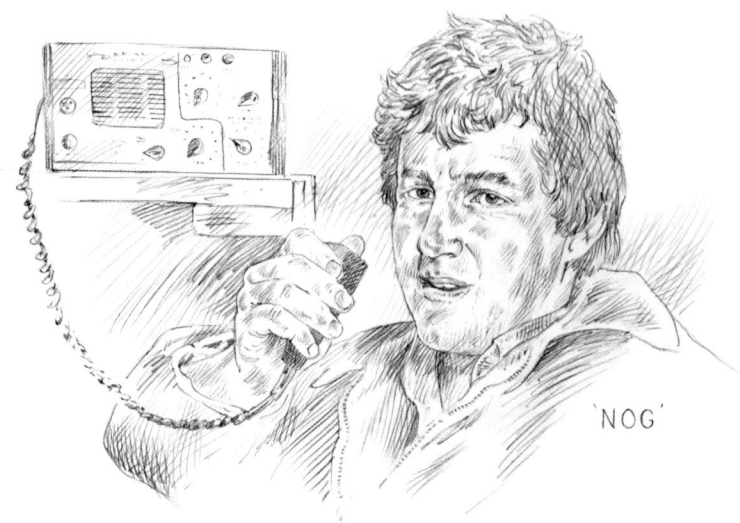

'NOG'

Nog is a field officer (Protected Fauna) who has done a four-year, in-the-field Wildlife trainee course and now works exclusively on wildlife listed in law as protected. Preparations for a field trip often seem more time consuming than the trip itself. Working out how much food six people will eat in three months is not too great a problem; working out how to transport the food to the Chathams is no great problem either; and getting fresh bread, vegetables and meat on the main Chatham Island while not too difficult, requires some local knowledge and organisation; but getting such perishables to the smaller islands is pure luck, and finally arriving on a remote island with everything one needs and all in working order seems to be impossible. Nog almost achieved the impossible. He remained with us only briefly at the beginning of the expedition to train us all in the finer points of tit nest management, returning later in the summer for a longer stay.

'NIGEL'

The hardest working members of the expedition — so they tell us — were Nigel Miller and Geordie Murman, both Wildlife trainees. They are expected to do almost anything, although, in fact, they were there to learn. Their four-year training course covers mountaineering, carpentry, ornithology and work in trout hatcheries, leaving some time for pastimes varying from squash to scuba-diving. Young, keen and fit, they worked hard, and their love of the underwater world kept us all well fed. For most of the trip Nigel worked with Don on Mangere while Geordie accompanied David and myself on South East Island.

'GEORDIE'

Fluffed out for insulation these two roosting warblers near our hut on South East Island looked more like powder puffs than birds. (Drawn by flashlight.)

Chatham Island Shag *Leucocarbo carunculatus onslowi*
This colonially breeding species appears to be present on Chatham, Pitt, South East, and a few smaller islands, all year round. The breeding season does not begin until November, but may vary from colony to colony. The 'chimney pot' nests are constructed from grass, seaweed and feathers firmly cemented together with droppings. Frequently, three eggs are laid but only one or two young reared. When just hatched the young are naked and resemble a deflated football bladder. One parent stays with them until they are well grown and covered in smoky brown down.

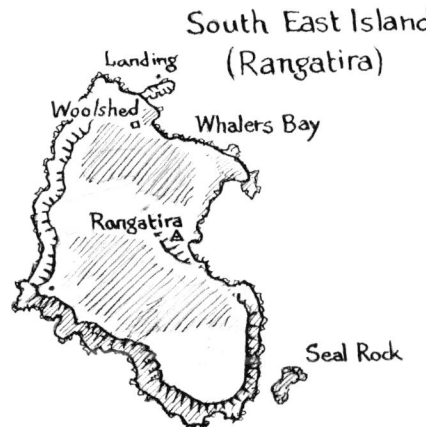

South East Island

SOUTH EAST ISLAND lies like a great wedge of a round cake laid on its side upon the sea with the 200-metre-high side facing the cold southerly winds, and the long sloping side to the sunny north.

Many years ago the Moriori probably visited South East Island to gather food, but no sign of their presence remains. A shore-based whaling station was established for a short period in the mid-1800s, and whales were hauled out on the naturally sloping rock platform of the bay now called Whaler's Bay. Any traces of the whaling station are now well buried in the tangle of muehlenbeckia vines and bracken that reach down to the storm line.

The first long-term, and more damaging, change was the introduction of Saxon Merino sheep which were brought to Pitt Island in 1842, and South East Island a few years later. At some stage goats were introduced, and by 1900 they had reached such numbers that sheep farming was no longer possible. Pigs may have been present too. In 1915 the grazing lease was renewed, the goats all shot, lowland areas of forest burnt, and pastures sown. During the following 40 years of farming there were some cattle, and sheep numbers varied from 700 to 1200.

One of the island's historic places is the woolshed — the only one on the island, probably built soon after 1915, and our home for this expedition. Originally it was designed for blade shearing, but was later equipped with machines and a woolpress to make full-sized bales rather than the lighter fadges used on some islands. Getting the bales down to the sea and into a boat must have required a fair degree of skill, and strength. In the last few years of farming twenty or so bales were the usual annual production of this 'one-farm' island. The woolshed also had the unusual addition of a fireplace as it was the only shelter for visiting shepherds and shearers. No one lived there permanently, however.

Elsewhere little evidence of farming remains: the occasional fence post, a sheep's skull, some pieces of number eight wire. The sheep dip — a necessary part of farming, even on an island — was built in a natural hole in the rock platform at the back of Whaler's Bay.

'SHEEP DIP'

Throughout this farming period, by good fortune, no mice, rats or cats got ashore, but land clearing had taken its toll. By 1954, when the island was declared a reserve for the preservation of flora and fauna, bird life was at a low ebb. Less than one third of the island still had forest cover and none of that had the shrubby understorey and ground cover plants so necessary for forest birds. Some forest birds had not been seen for many years and nesting seabirds were almost gone.

The grazing lease expired in 1957. Most of the sheep and cattle were taken off by 1959, and the remaining sheep were removed in 1961.

Forest regeneration on the island has been remarkable, as has the increase in bird numbers. All the bird species recorded by ornithologists as long ago as 1871 are still present. Until recently two of these — the shore plover

Facing page: Not far from the woolshed David found this fine view over Whaler's Bay to Pitt Island and the distinctive hill called 'Walkemup'. In earlier times, horses could not be ridden up the steep slopes, so shepherds had to 'walk them up'.

and the snipe — were found only on South East Island (snipe have now been transferred to Mangere Island), and for seven other endemic species of Chatham Island birds this island is the only stronghold. Six of these birds are so rare that they are considered to be endangered. Additionally, in retrospect, we might reasonably suspect that the Chatham Island pigeon, Forbes parakeet and black robin must have been and gone before the first ornithologists arrived. The pigeon and Forbes parakeet still exist on other islands — albeit precariously — and the Wildlife Service has recently moved black robins to South East Island. It was to help the black robin, the rarest of the rare, with just one pair on South East Island, that we travelled there. Our main task was to find tit nests and prepare them to foster eggs which we would take from the black robin nests here and on Mangere Island.

Air transport may well have improved access to the main Chatham islands but getting to the outliers such as South East is still an adventure. Chatham Island weather is too windy for boating every day and the fishermen have a relatively short crayfishing season, so they need all the income they can get. When we come along wanting to get to remote islands and can offer only a half day's pay for a full day's work we are understandably squeezed in when the weather and fishing permit. Often this results in last minute plan changes and night trips in boats designed neither for passengers nor baggage, over seas that are far from smooth. In the fisherman's world only the capable survive so we are assured of safe delivery to our islands. Without the fishermen nothing would have been achieved.

Landing on island shores is usually done by small dinghy. Very rarely is it possible for a larger boat to come in close. In a few places the island rock is shaped like a wharf and it was to one such 'wharf' that our boatman, Tony Anderson, brought us. Coming ashore in the black of night should be considered nothing less than a bad dream!

The next day, at the same rocky wharf, the work began: three months' stores and equipment was passed piece by piece from the hold, around the wheelhouse, along the bow, to the shore, and then high enough up the rocks to avoid the next high tide. A crate of oranges, car battery, roll of polythene, solar panel, 60-litre drum of petrol, sacks of potatoes, camp beds, incubator, brightly painted expedition boxes, cartons and cartons of food and lots, lots more. It all had to be shifted to the old woolshed.

The old woolshed has been the working base on the island since the reserve was created, but now the 'old' is more descriptive than 'woolshed'. The route to it leads from the waterhole on the shore where the skuas and red-billed gulls like to bathe, up to the next rock platform, with pools for the parakeets and tuis, and into the forest. A short way along a slightly winding track through the trees can be seen a corrugated iron wall — more rust than galvanising, and clearly depending for support more on the trees than its framework.

Facing page: The entrance to the woolshed — our home on South East Island.

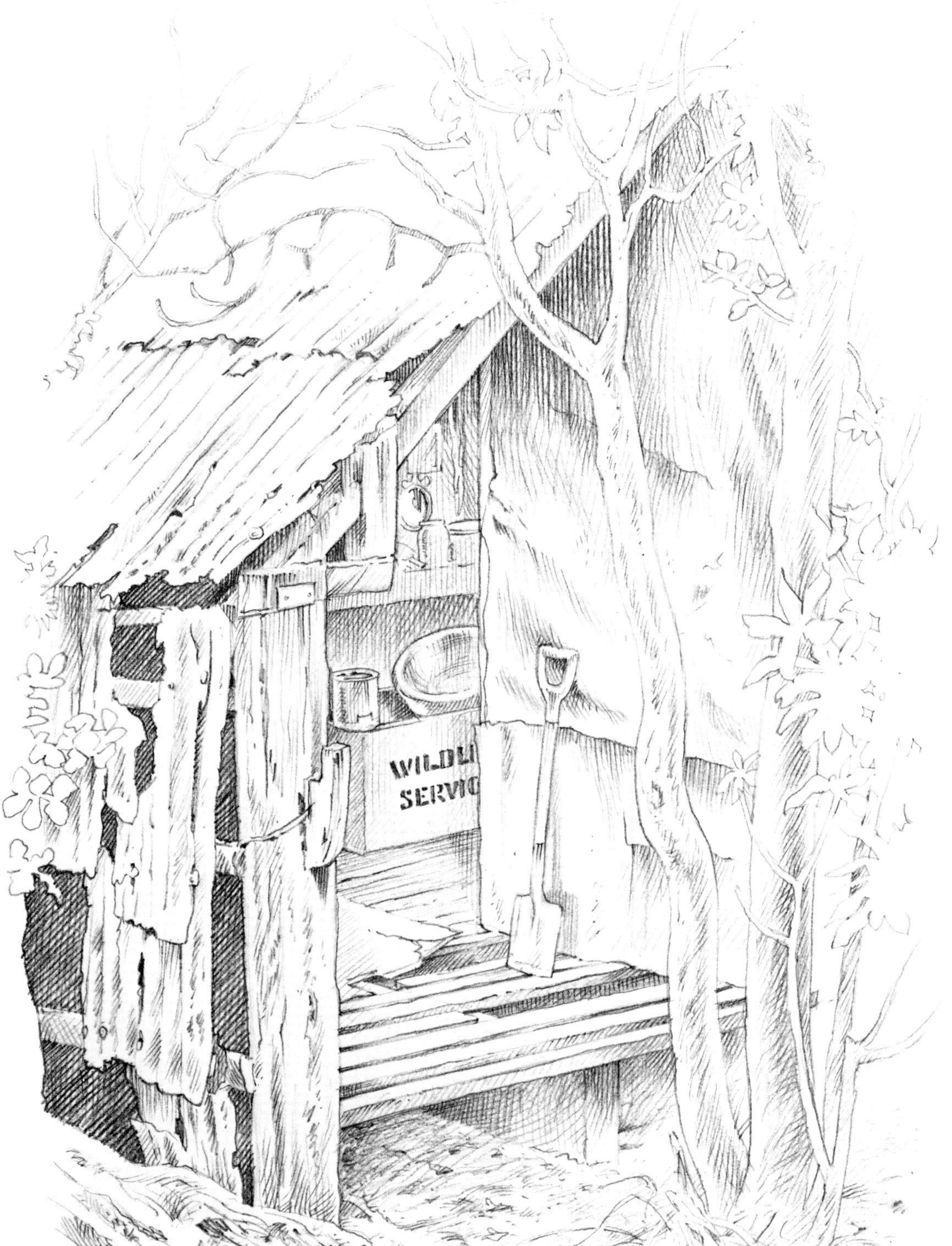
WILDLI
SERVIC

Inside was no better. The floor sloped away from the drier centre to the rotten outer piles. A broad-billed prion was nesting in the long-disused fireplace, another in the old woolpress, one under the makeshift cooking bench, another on some blue plastic in the corner and, as we learned after dark, hundreds under the floor. Outside a gap in the wall a previous visitor had placed half a fishing float as a bird bath. Inside the roof, tent flies had been strung up to divert most of the rain water.

Writing on some of the remaining wall boards testified to previous occupancy: 'Sea Devil Hough July 1937' and 'S. Hough shipwrecked 27/2/1983' stood out from the faded words. In bold black on one board the entire length of the shed the words 'Palmer & Co, Artists, Photographers, Taxidermists and Bird Stuffers' were a grim reminder of the earlier killing and commercialised collecting of rare birds. This was our home.

As our sojourn continued we learned quickly that, rather than sleeping inside the woolshed, we could have a better night's sleep by pitching our tent outside, away from the mass of prions: so silent by day, but a chorus of raucous love songsters by night. Individuals or pairs in their natural place in burrows were much quieter than that under-floor commune.

For our comfort in the woolshed 'living room' Geordie used most of our roll of polythene, pinned up with hundreds of staples, to reduce the flow of cold southerly air and divert the rainwater a little further toward the edges of the floor space.

Our 'in-use' provisions were stored on makeshift shelves. The rest were left in their cartons and stacked in suitable places. The carton of toilet paper became a table, the box of office papers, a chair. In this climate there was no need for a fridge for eggs, butter or cheese, and to help our bread and cabbages last, these were hung on strings in an airy corner of the room.

For meat we had brought half a sheep. It too should have been hung in that airy corner, but the kind butcher had cut it into cooking pieces and the meat had spent a few days packed in plastic bags. There was little we could do but eat it fast. After that there was no fresh red meat. Tinned meat is really best kept for emergencies or, in other camps, the dog. So we survived, very happily, on a diet of fresh blue cod, paua and crayfish until Geordie decided a change was needed and made a deal with Ken Lanauze, our nearest neighbour, on Pitt Island, for some fresh meat. Pitt Islanders usually have no market for their meat so the chance to trade was welcomed and a huge lump of steak was delivered.

Fuel was stored on the few remaining gratings of the old sheep pens. Nowadays we need quite a range: petrol, kerosene, meths and various oils. Since, in the best interests of the reserve, we stopped chopping firewood many years ago, we have used kerosene-fuelled, double-burner primus stoves for cooking. Lighting systems are varied and in recent years have undergone considerable change. We used to have just a Tilley lamp, but with the advent of larger radios for contact with the mainland, and the need

Facing page: One of the many broad-billed prions nesting under the floorboards of the woolshed.

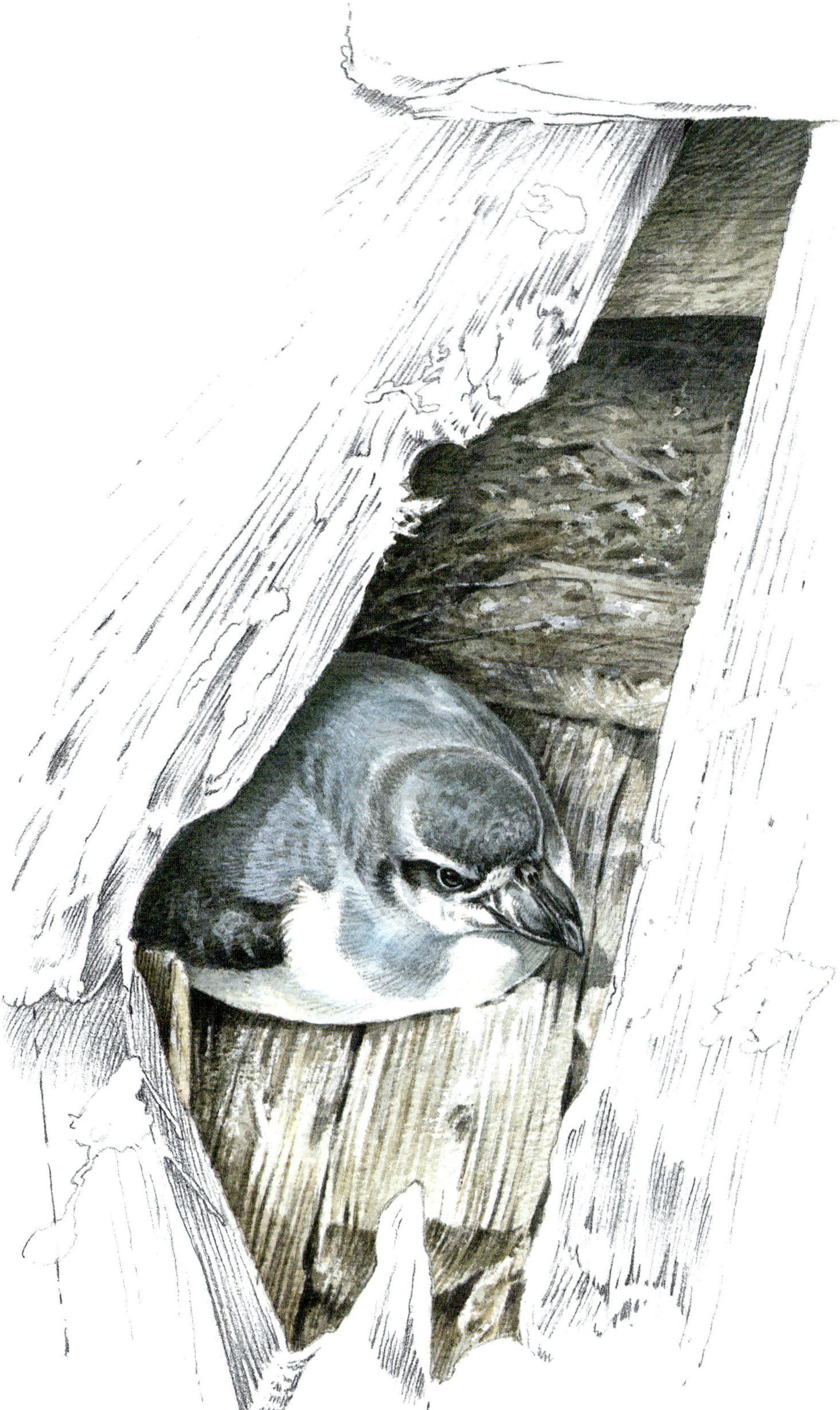

for rechargeable batteries for them and other work, we have been using small portable generators. Now, because the generator is available, household lights are being used in many camps. This in turn means that we have to carry more fuel and put up with the noise of a generator all evening. I thought I was smart enough to do away with all that by using the wonderful new technology of a solar panel. It went well for the first two weeks but then failed miserably in a week of low cloud and rain. Eventually, our generator failed too so we returned to Tilley lamp, candles and early bed.

Few people who live in suburbia give much thought to their water supply except when the bill arrives. Most of our more permanent work-places are huts with a rainwater tank, or stream nearby. Here in the woolshed, however, spoutings were long gone and most of the rainfall soaked easily into the friable soil, so we had to go down to the forest edge where the water seeped out over the bedrock. A series of plastic tubes (originally supplied to carry bird bands) lashed to an old flax flower stem, made an excellent pipeline to divert the 'guano rich' water into our container.

Most of our work on South East Island was with the Chatham Island tits and black robins not far from the woolshed. To minimise environmental damage we marked the two main tracks through the bush with pieces of red plastic tape.

Outwardly the bush on the island looks like many other areas of forest regenerating naturally after years of grazing: large areas of trees, some old ones falling down, patches of grass, some ferns, and many young trees. Inside the forest it is quite different, for this is a seabird-nesting island. Wherever the soil is the right texture the ground is riddled with the burrows of nesting prions and petrels. The owners of these burrows return at night to swap places with an incubating mate, or feed a waiting chick. The bark on sloping trees is worn smooth by the birds climbing to gain elevation for take-off back to sea. Occasionally, those that miss the 'launch tree' may be found at daybreak, but usually they are easy prey for skuas, gulls and the occasional harrier.

It is the younger trees that show the signs of recent regeneration. After the removal of the sheep these fast growers shot skywards towards the holes in the forest canopy. Now, with their equally upright branches, and acutely angled forks, they are traps for many prions. Fortunately, that cycle has nearly passed and the next generation of trees is more like those of a hundred years ago, with slower growth and wide-spreading branches.

South East Island now is a haven for wildlife: by day the forest and its scrubby margins contain fifteen bird species; by night eight species of seabird fly, fall, or walk in; and around the coast live another eight. It is almost the same as it was when man first arrived.

Facing page: Shore plovers feeding along the edges of one of the many rock pools on South East Island.

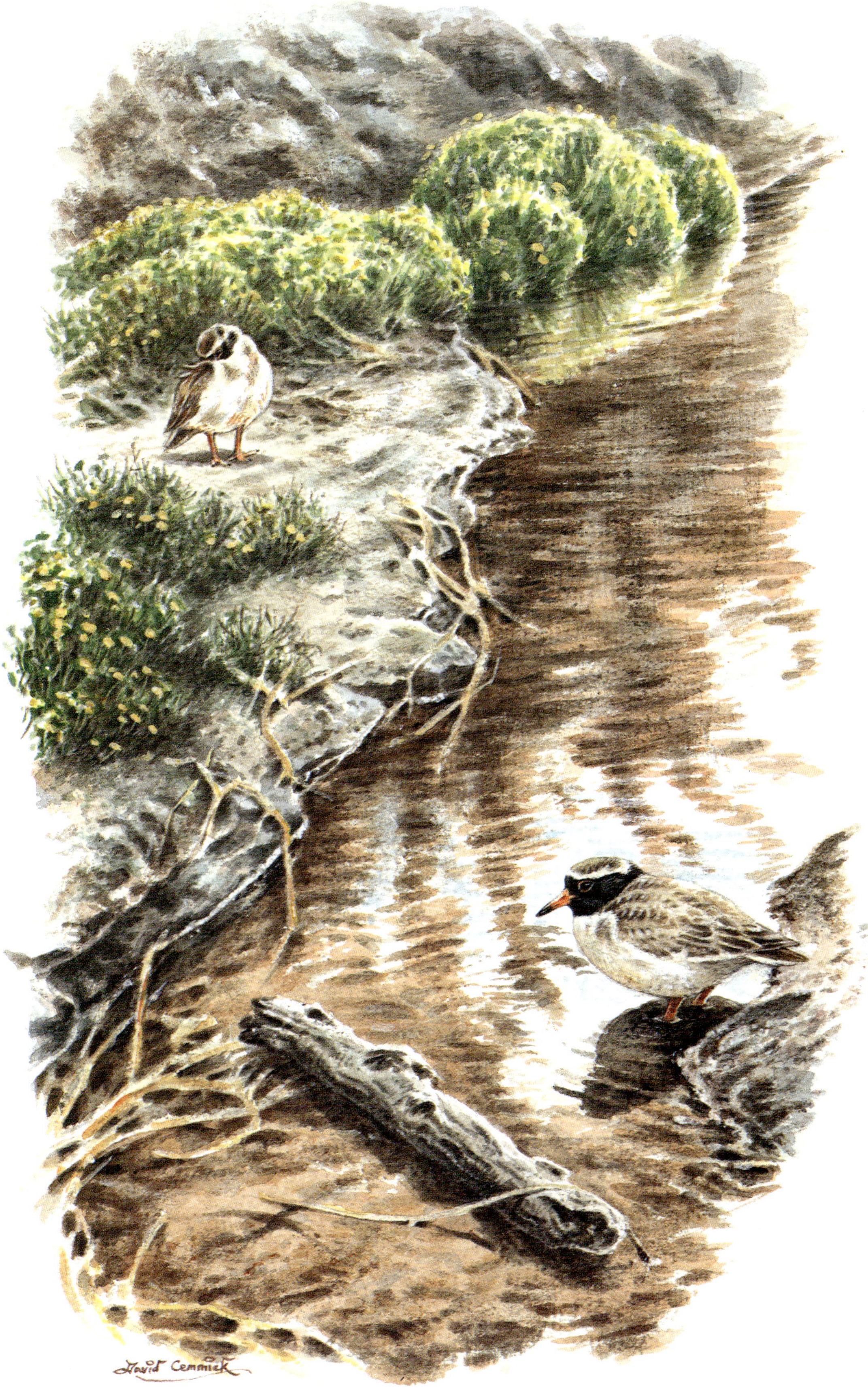
David Cemmick

Broad-Billed Prion *Pachyptila vittata vittata*
This is by far the most abundant seabird nesting in the forests of Mangere and South East islands. No one has ever tried to estimate how many hundreds of thousands there are. Usually, they nest in burrows in the ground — a pair to a burrow — but they also squeeze into every suitable nook and cranny: holes in logs, big cavities in standing trees, under boulders, and every corner of the woolshed — indeed, any hiding place that will keep them out of sight of the ever hungry skuas.

    Both birds of a pair share the incubation of a single egg for the 56 days it takes to hatch. We were amazed to see that the egg in the woolshed fireplace was left unincubated for at least three days, yet hatched successfully a few days later.

    The bills of the prion family are a lesson in evolution. They vary in size from the narrow bill of the fairy prion to the shovel shape of the broad-billed prion, each adapted to take advantage of a particular food source.

Above: Broad-billed prion chick at 14 days.
Facing page: The chick being brooded by its parent in the woolpress.

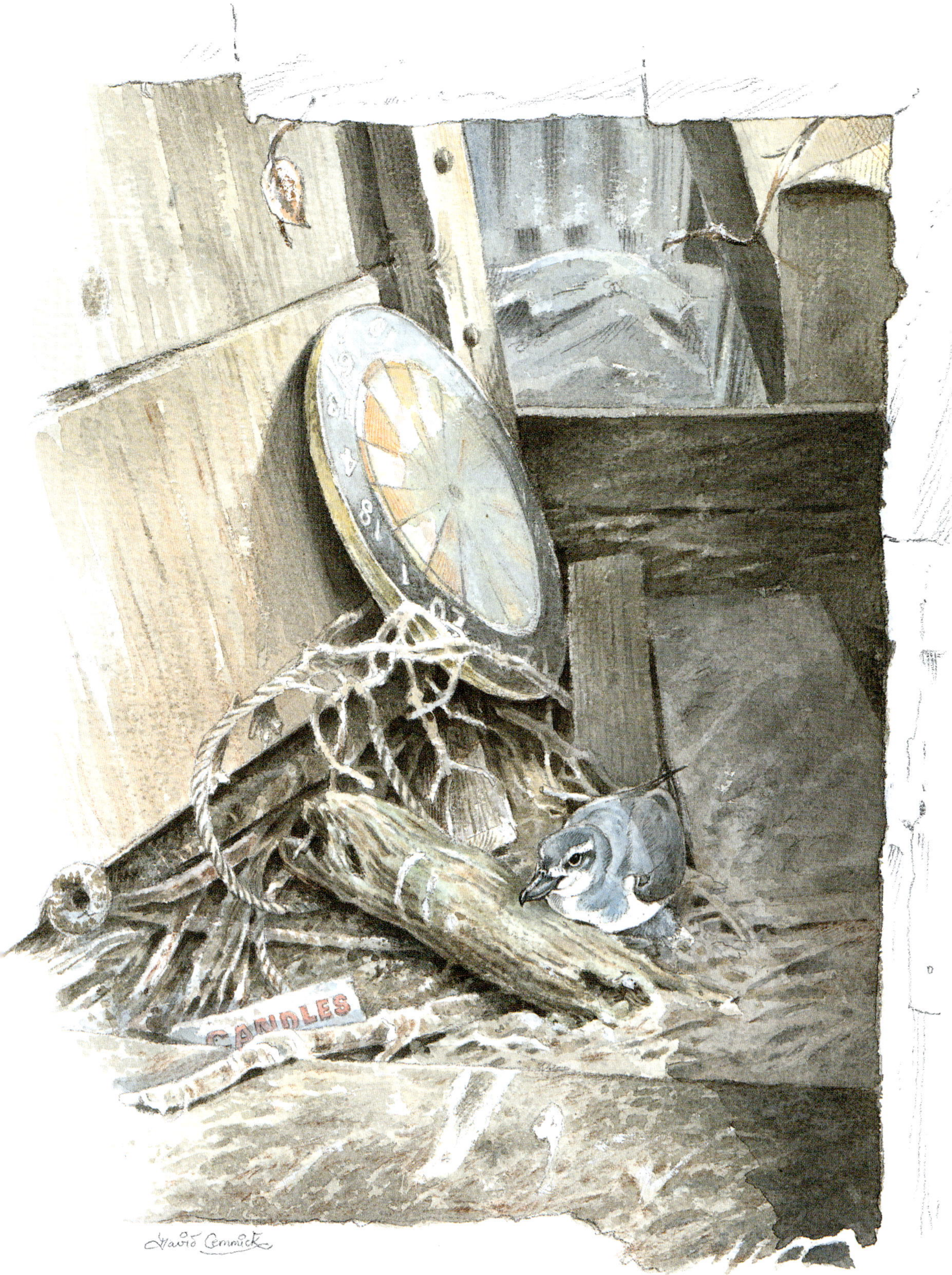
CANDLES
David Cemmick

Broad billed prion headstudies

BROAD BILLED PRION HUNG BY THE NECK IN THE FORK OF A BRANCH WHILST CRASHING THROUGH THE TREE CANOPY ON ROUTE TO ITS NESTING BURROW. 1·11·83.

Above: Where the soil is suitable the forest floor is a myriad of seabird burrows: mostly those of broad-billed prions, but penguins, storm petrels, diving petrels, and the rare Chatham Island petrel, can all find spaces. Every large tree that slopes a bit is used as a launching pad by birds that need to gain height to start their return flight to the sea.

Petrels

The small petrels — the grey-backed storm, white-faced storm and diving species — are just a few of the smallest members of a vast, world-wide family of seabirds. Their biggest relative is the giant petrel with a two metre wing-span. At sea the white-faced storm petrel is one of our better known birds. Its habit of skipping and dancing with its feet frequently touching the water has earned it the name 'Jesus Christ bird'.

These species spend most of the year at sea, but during the breeding season return to their nest burrows at night. During this period they can fall prey to patrolling skuas. The diving petrel evades the predators by flying at great speed, with an uncanny ability to fly directly to its burrow without hitting any trees. The grey-backed storm petrel carefully makes its burrow under dense vegetation, but the white-faced storm petrel seems to take no special precautions, fluttering lightly down through the forest canopy to within a few metres of 'home'.

Grey-backed storm petrel and Diving petrel head studies showing bill and head shapes. 28/29.10.83.

I drew this grey backed storm petrel as it fluttered feebly over the grass near the woolshed seeking cover.

Grey-backed Storm Petrel

White faced storm petrel sitting in the warmth of Dicks hand whilst he talked on the radio
8.45p.m 24.10.84

Overall very dark brown plumage with glossy sheen.
Underside white — feet and legs vivid sky blue.

10·30 p.m 24th Oct. I picked this Diving Petrel up outside the woolshed and brought it inside to sketch — it was totally unconcerned and fell asleep!

White faced Storm Petrels.
— woolshed - 10.30 p.m 27.10.83.

Eggs of seabirds: *from left,* broad-billed prion; diving petrel; grey-backed storm petrel; white-faced storm petrel.

51

Facing page: David removed the 'shackles' from the legs of this white-faced storm petrel and let it go, but for many more birds the shackle means death.

The shackle is a chain of hundreds of tiny trematode worms accidentally joined together and, equally accidentally, wrapped around the petrel's legs. The resultant death of the petrel is of no benefit to the worms.

Full details of the life of the trematode, *Distomum filiferum,* are not known. It seems that as an egg, or when very young, one will get into the body cavity of a small oceanic shrimp. When it has grown to four or five millimetres in length it leaves the shrimp and drifts in the sea awaiting an opportunity to attach itself, by its long sticky filaments, to a larger host, presumably a fish, where it either grows further or develops eggs. The long sticky filaments, while being very necessary appendages, are also the cause of its downfall, for they tangle with the filaments of other trematodes and, in due course, a chain is formed. Some of these become attached to the legs of petrels.

Most white-faced storm petrels have a trematode anklet around one or both legs, but only a few have them joined as a shackle. While we could not find these on other petrel species, they apparently do occur but have not been known to form the fatal shackle.

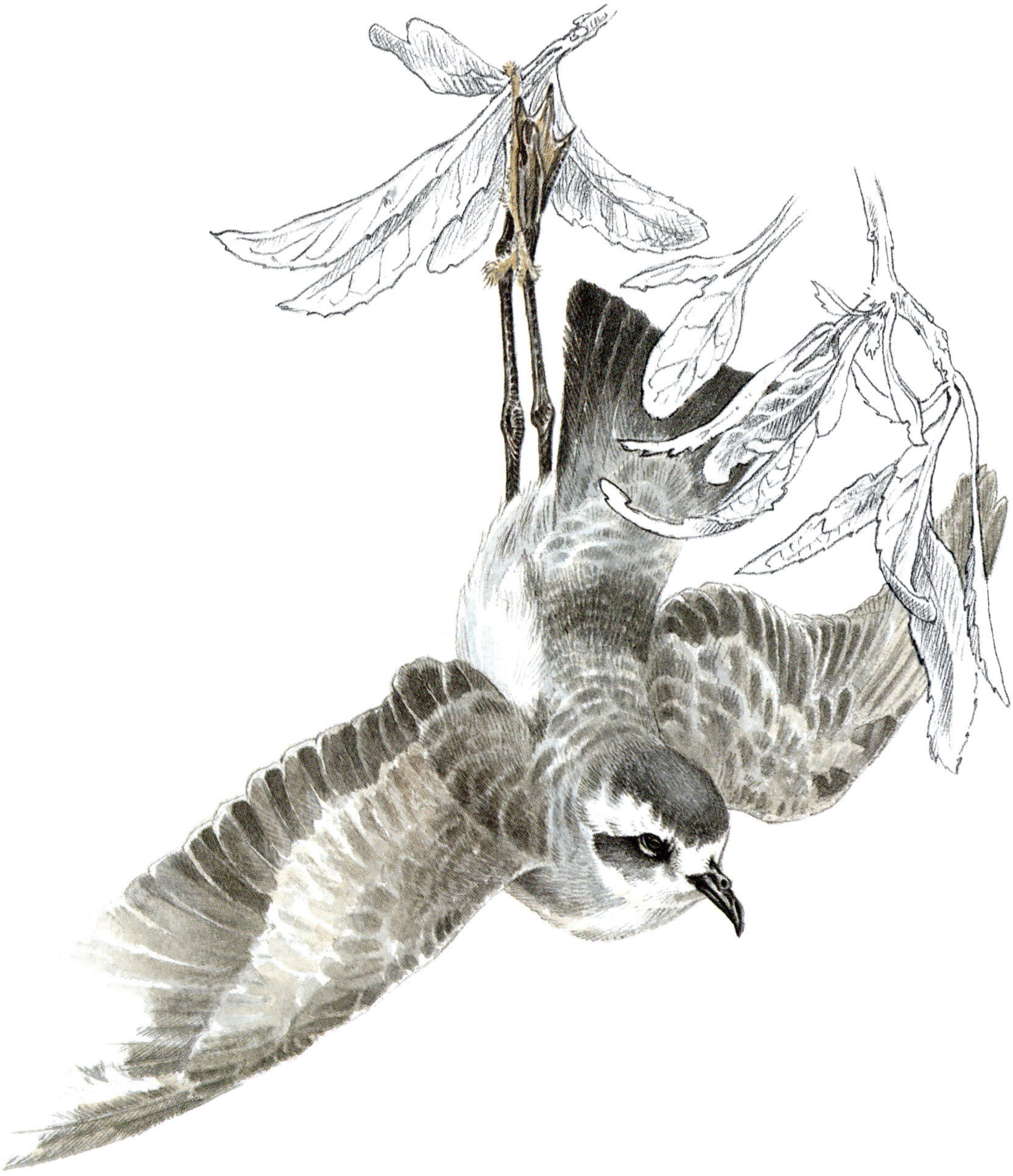

'BLUE COD'

FEEDING A COD
WITH LIMPET.

GEORDIE CAUGHT SEVERAL COD AND PLACED THEM
IN A LARGE ROCKPOOL IN WHALERS BAY. IT
TOOK ONLY A FEW DAYS BEFORE THEY WOULD
FEED STRAIGHT FROM OUR HANDS.

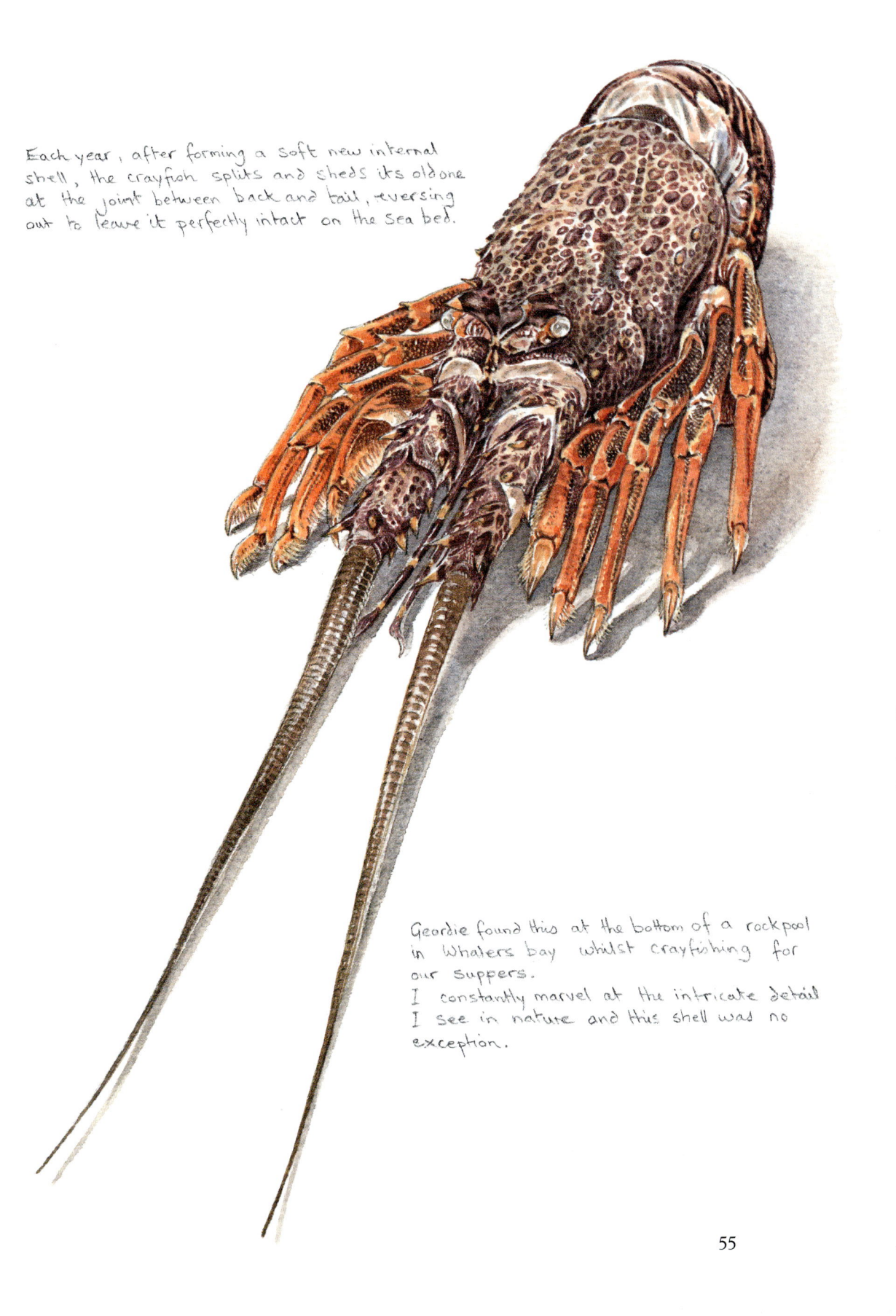

Each year, after forming a soft new internal shell, the crayfish splits and sheds its old one at the joint between back and tail, eversing out to leave it perfectly intact on the sea bed.

Geordie found this at the bottom of a rockpool in Whalers bay whilst crayfishing for our suppers.
I constantly marvel at the intricate detail I see in nature and this shell was no exception.

Sketches of Redbilled gulls at the nest.

Pale cream iris
Blood red eye ring,
bill and feet.

A twelve foot long Elephant Seal resting from
the sun in a rockpool in Whalers Bay.
It went to sleep with its nostrils submerged
for fifteen minutes at a time between breaths.

Drawn between 1.00 – 5.30 p.m 24·10·83.

'chattering'

Scraping meulinbecia leaves.

Female 'food begging' from male.

They may appear a very vivid green here — though parakeets in their natural environment, amongst the sun dappled leaf canopy, are extremely difficult to spot. Listening for their chattering contact calls helped me locate feeding birds.

Chatham Island Red-Crowned Parakeet
Cyanoramphus novaezelandiae chathamensis

Larger, and apparently more adaptable, than the yellow-crowned parakeet, the red-crowned species has successfully occupied many man-modified habitats, as long as there are holes left to nest in. It is now a very common bird on both Mangere and South East islands.

Red crowned parakeet feeding on watercress.

♂ Generally larger and more intense green with deeper red more clearly defined than female.
♀ More sombre with untidy plumage, shorter tail and smaller bill with more blue showing on wings than male.

Chatham Island Fantail *Rhipidura fuliginosa penitus*
The taxonomists have described very carefully how the Chatham Island fantail has more white on its tail than its mainland counterpart. Only after much observation was it possible to record these differences and support their findings. By mid-November there were many young fantails constantly begging for food which the male fantail continued to supply while the female prepared a new nest for the next brood. If the weather is good two, or even three, broods may be successfully raised by a pair in one summer.

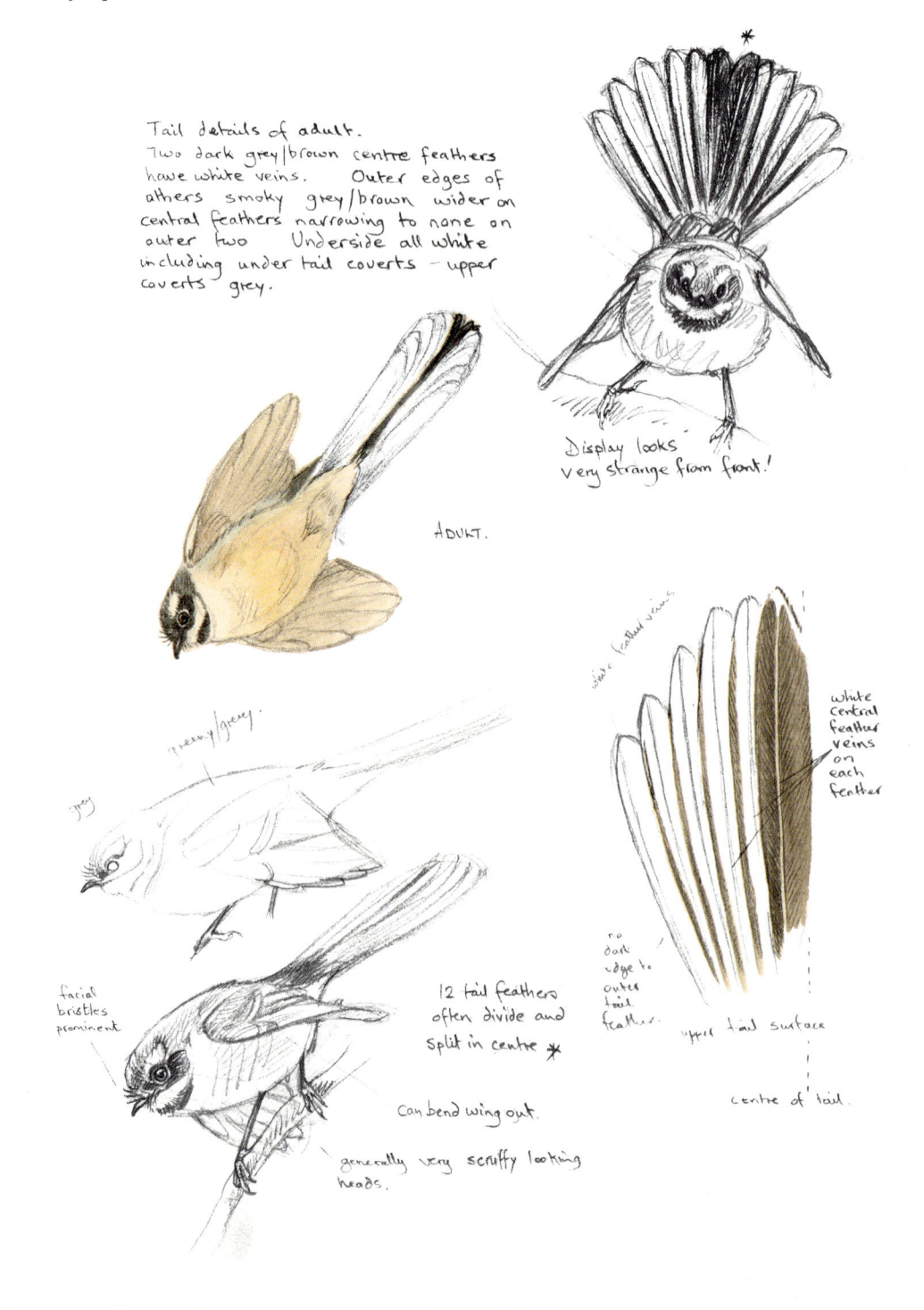

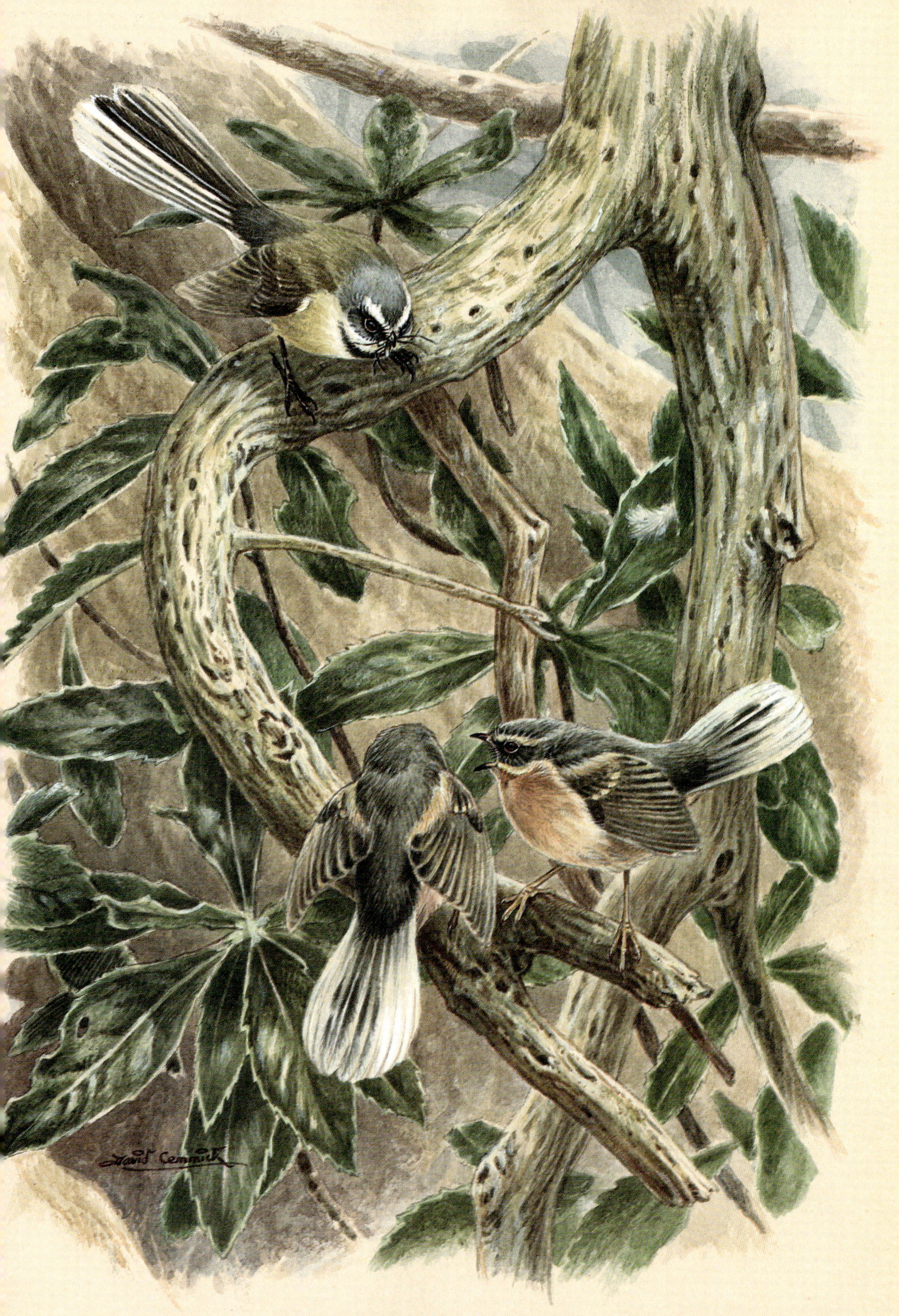

I stood on a ladder to sketch this fantail nest which had been built twelve feet high in a Myrsine chathamica tree.   S.E. Island 7·11·83.

Chatham Island Fantail
Adult and juvenile studies

adult

grey tint to sides of chest

head very small

shape when not displaying.

ADULT.

dk chestnut/olive back. upper t. cov grey/green.

under t. cov white.

inside secondaries edged warm yellow ochre.

adult legs dark.

adult tail length
juv tail length

food begging.

dull lemon chest with salmon tint. adult whitish

JUVENILE

upper tail coverts dark grey

buff tint

wings often open

adult territorial display.

base to bill pink tip dk.

grey head showing faint pale throat line & eye stripe.

pink breast

orange/pink feet & legs.

juv tail shorter than adult. with grey mottling.

four cream tips to sec/coverts

in juvenile tail = body length.

David Emmett

The Fostering Project

AFTER THE SUCCESSFUL transfer in 1976 of the entire black robin population from the degenerating forest on Little Mangere Island to the regenerating forest on Mangere Island, there was no attempt to alter or assist the birds' breeding.

In the spring of that year just one chick was raised and one adult had died, so the total population remained at seven. The following year with two chicks raised and two adults having died, the population was still seven. In 1978 one chick was raised but three birds died, so the population dropped to five, and in 1979 another chick was raised and another bird died, so the total black robin population remained at five.

Clearly the robins were not producing enough young to replace themselves. Their productivity needed to be boosted. Left alone, each pair would spend three months, nearly the whole summer, attempting to rear one, or very rarely two, chicks. Then there was not enough summer left for them to try again.

Nest building and egg laying, however, takes only the first few weeks of this time so, if the eggs could be taken away soon after laying, there would be plenty of time for a second clutch, or even a third, to be laid and a chick reared. This is the sort of cycle that occurs if a nest is lost to natural causes, so it would not harm the birds if we simulated the loss.

The problem then was how to raise chicks from the 'stolen' eggs. Aviary rearing was out of the question so thoughts were turned towards fostering, whereby birds naturally, but unknowingly, rear chicks for other birds. On Mangere Island possible foster parents are the Chatham Island warbler and the less abundant introduced hedge sparrow which both rear the young of the shining cuckoo. It was soon found that the warblers were excellent parents, taking good care of the chicks of other species put into their nests by man.

The fostering birds also tolerated manipulations of their nests. In experiments it was established that a warbler's nest, over a period of days,

Above: Black robin.
Facing page: Chatham Island warbler studies.

♂

♀

After feeding their chicks either adult would sometimes wait to extract a faecal sack before flying well away from the nest with it.

These chicks were nearly fully fledged.

David Cemmick

could be moved some distance from its original location. This proved to be very useful in making nests more secure or to bring them down to our working level. Swapping eggs was no problem either: big eggs or small, the warbler accepted them all. A major difficulty was getting the eggs through the small entrance of a warbler nest. By modifying a plastic milk-powder spoon for its fragile cargo we were able to slip it easily through the nest entrance.

Unfortunately, after all this experimentation, we found that, for no apparent reason, the robin chicks were dying in the warbler's nest when ten days old. Even changing the whole nest for a new clean one did not solve the problem.

We also provided the robins with some nest boxes which, fortunately, they like to use. Strong nest boxes are much safer, and make finding and manipulating the robin nests much easier.

The spring of 1980 was therefore a complex series of nest, egg and chick swapping. At that stage there were only two female robins, recognised by their colour bands as 'Green' and 'Blue'.

The season began with Blue laying two eggs. These were put in warbler's nests; only one hatched but the chick died when ten days old. Green started her first clutch five days after Blue. These were also put in warbler's nests and one hatched. By this time Blue had laid again but instead of just taking her eggs away to a warbler's nest they were replaced by Green's chick, now ten days old and in imminent danger of dying if left in the warbler's nest. Green laid again and hatched one chick. By this time the two chicks from Blue's second clutch were approaching their tenth day in a warbler's nest but there were no spaces available in a nest where they could be reared to fledging in this serious game of musical nests. If left as they were, Blue's two chicks were sure to die and Green's second chick live. So they were swapped and Blue's two chicks lived.

Thus, in the spring of 1980, three chicks were raised. That was quite a success, but a rather risky way of improving productivity. Better ways had to be found. A better, more compatible foster parent perhaps?

A more suitable foster parent would most likely be found amongst relatives of the black robin, as relatives often have similar habits. Within the Chatham Islands, the Chatham Island tit is the black robin's closest relative. There were no tits on Mangere Island but, fortunately, plenty in the forests of South East Island.

Many of the nest boxes have had words or phrases added to accompany their identification numbers. I thought this was suitably reverent for a black robin nest!

Chatham Island Warbler *Gerygone albofrontata*
The Chatham Island warbler is for ever on the move — searching for insects, singing, preening, nest building. Indeed, it builds what must be the warmest nest in the forest. Grasses and fibres are patiently bound together with spiders' webs to form the almost totally enclosed nest. Inside are hundreds of downy feathers which, until the growing chicks tramp them down, seem to fill the nest cavity. It is little wonder then, that for the first few days after leaving such a warm place, newly fledged chicks, like the one opposite, constantly squeak and beg for food.

juvenile pink feet and bill, eye black, lemon around.
adult grey/brown feet and bill.

Juvenile —
Grey head and chest
Nape, face and throat pale grey but with brown tinge.
Back brown, upper tail coverts sienna.
Body cream/white with faint striations.
Throat has lemon tinge.
Strong lemon eye stripe.

Except when dozing after a large feed juveniles are constantly pecking:— leaves, passing flies, its feathers, toes or the perch its sitting on! They also scratch, stretch and preen a lot.

'TUG OF WAR'
— WARBLER FEEDING.

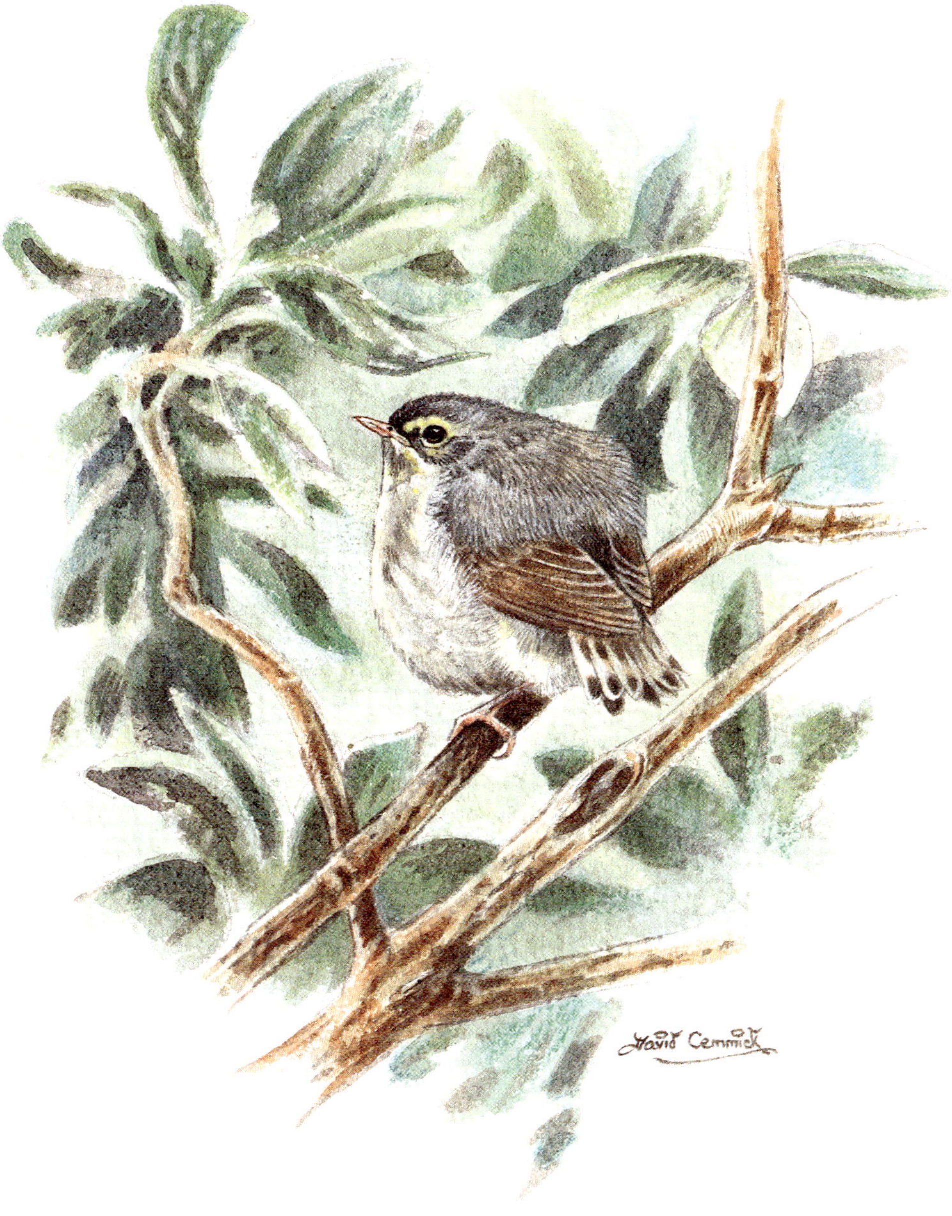
David Cemmick

The Foster Parents

TO USE TIT nests as foster homes for black robins we had to find each nest very early in the sequence of nest building so that we could then choose and manipulate nests to suit the timing of the development of the robin egg. Each nest was given an identification number, and a tag bearing this number was placed near the nest.

The Chatham Island tit is a little larger than its mainland counterpart, with the male having bolder breast colouring. All year he defends a forest territory for himself and his lifelong mate. When the breeding season begins the female chooses a nest site amongst vines, or in a shallow cavity in a tree trunk, and there builds a nest of filamentous material bound with cobwebs. She partly lines the nest and leaves it for a week or more before the first egg is laid.

During the course of laying the eggs — one a day until she has a full clutch of three or four — she adds feathers and a little moss. The female alone then incubates the eggs for 17 to 18 days. During the nest building and incubation the male provides all or most of her food. When the chicks hatch he feeds only them while the female returns to feeding herself as well as sharing the feeding of the chicks.

To make the tit nest site as safe as possible for the black robin eggs and chicks, modifications were occasionally needed. If the tangle of vines near the nest was too thick, a hand-sized pathway would have to be cleared. If exposed to rain, a plastic roof could be added or, in fragile sites, poles and string used for extra strength. These changes were best made in the period between nest building and egg laying.

Later, the number of eggs in the nest would have to be reduced, one egg at a time, to two. This is so that the later swap to two robin eggs, or

Above: A female Chatham Island tit collecting lace bark, a favourite material for nest building. South East Island 13.11.83.

one robin and one plastic, would not be too much of a change. By this time, because we had fed him each time we met, the male tit was usually easily attracted to human sounds; he would be fed a large grub and would, in turn, call the female off the nest. We could then take or swap eggs without unduly disturbing her.

Indeed, any changes which could possibly benefit the black robin chicks were tried, even if this meant the sacrifice of tit eggs or the destruction of a nest to force renesting in a better site. We found great variety in the temperament of the tit pairs: some would tolerate significant changes to their nest sites; some would regularly make excellent, safe nests; others would make flimsy nests and desert easily.

For short shifts robin eggs were carried in warmed containers lined with cotton wool, but between islands a custom-built portable incubator was used. Each move was arranged with care and contingency plans.

Whenever possible two or three tit nests were prepared for the robin eggs. The female robin would be called from her nest in the same manner as the female tit. Then her eggs would be lifted carefully from the nest with the special egg spoon and replaced with plastic ones just in case we needed to return her own eggs. Only after watching the foster parent tit for long enough to be very sure that she had accepted her new charges would we remove the robin's nest so that she would start the nesting cycle again

I counted 124 feathers in this deserted tit nest. There were 112 Broad billed Prion; 6 Tui; 2 Storm Petrel; 2 Red crowned Parakeet; 1 Starling and the unusual inclusion of a single snipe feather.

and produce two or three more eggs, just as she would if her nest had been destroyed by some natural event.

Eventually, most tit foster parents had just one egg each, for even the nests we judged as very safe could be tipped up by a landing petrel or hit by a falling branch. Robin eggs, which are slightly larger than tit eggs, take about 18 days to hatch, then it is a further 22 days before the chick — nearly the same size as a tit chick — leaves the nest. After that it still depends on its parents — for 30 days if cared for by a tit or 40 days if with robin parents. As they mature the robins appear to forget their tit foster parents and look only for black robins as mates.

Above: A female Chatham Island tit incubating four eggs. The nest was built in the top of an old *Olearia traversi* stump, four metres above the ground.

The male brings food to the female during incubation, calling her twenty or thirty yards from the nestsite to be fed. One female I timed took only fifteen seconds to fly thirty yards from the nest, receive food, fly back and be re-settled in incubation.

We fed the tits on small wetas, white grubs and cockroaches.

Above: Chatham Island tit studies.
Facing page: Both male and female tit share the feeding of their young. The male is carrying a faecal sac from the nest.

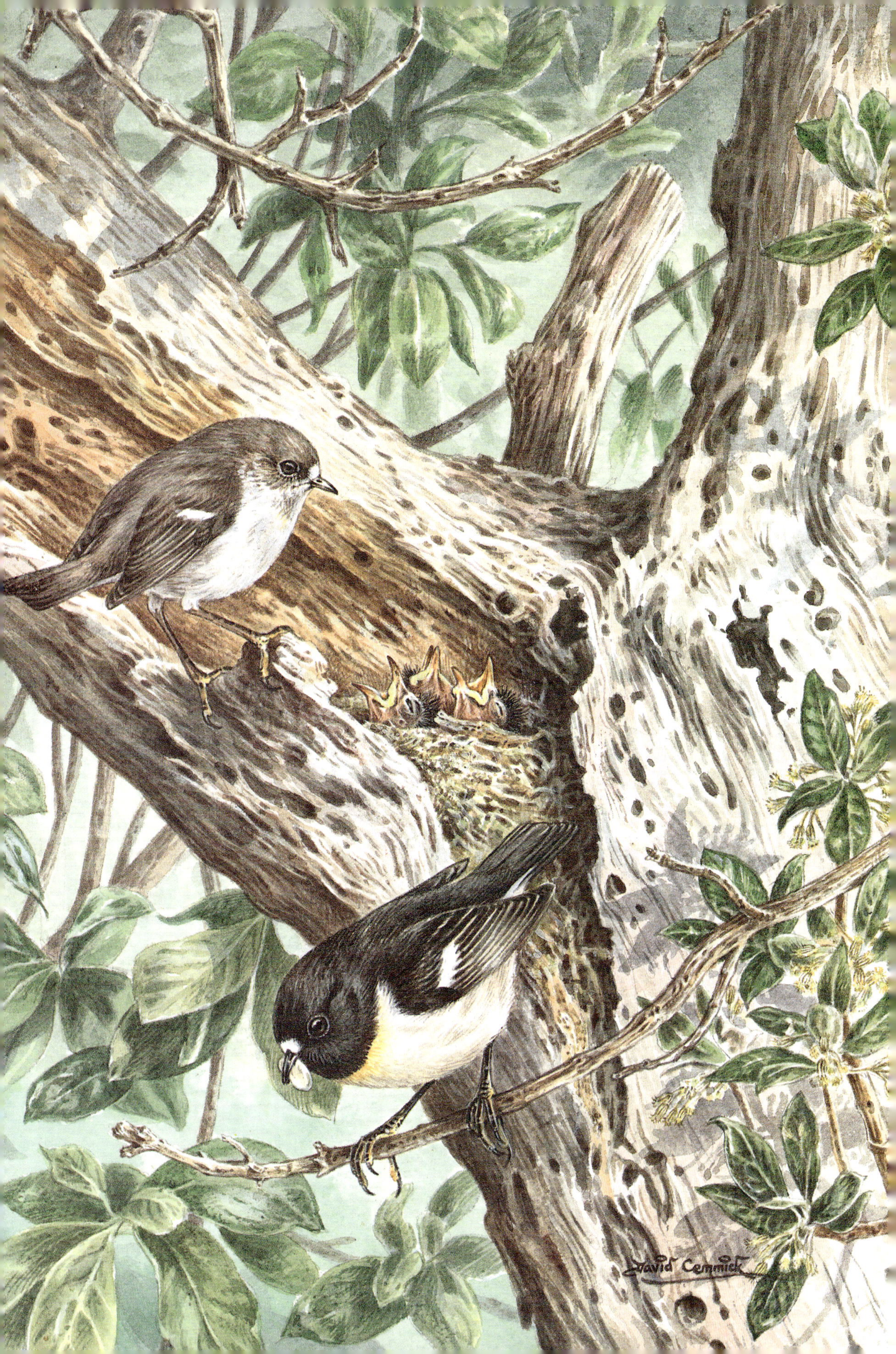
David Cemmick

chick

THAM ISLAND SNIPE EGG
ACTUAL SIZE

Chatham Island Snipe   *Coenocorypha aucklandica pusilla*
This quietly confident little bird of the forest floor and shrubland was once found throughout the Chatham Islands, but with the introduction of predators by Europeans it disappeared from all islands except South East. The Wildlife Service has recently successfully reintroduced it to Mangere Island. Nests are well hidden, usually under clumps of grass, but, just to show how prone to predation this species is, humans can, with care, approach the nest and stroke the sitting bird. The small downy young — often only one and rarely more than two — leave the nest soon after hatching and follow their parents closely. The adults search for insects among the leaf litter and frequently probe with their bills deep into the soil. Territorial defence is usually achieved by calling, but if a close encounter occurs, a mock sword-fight with bills may take place.

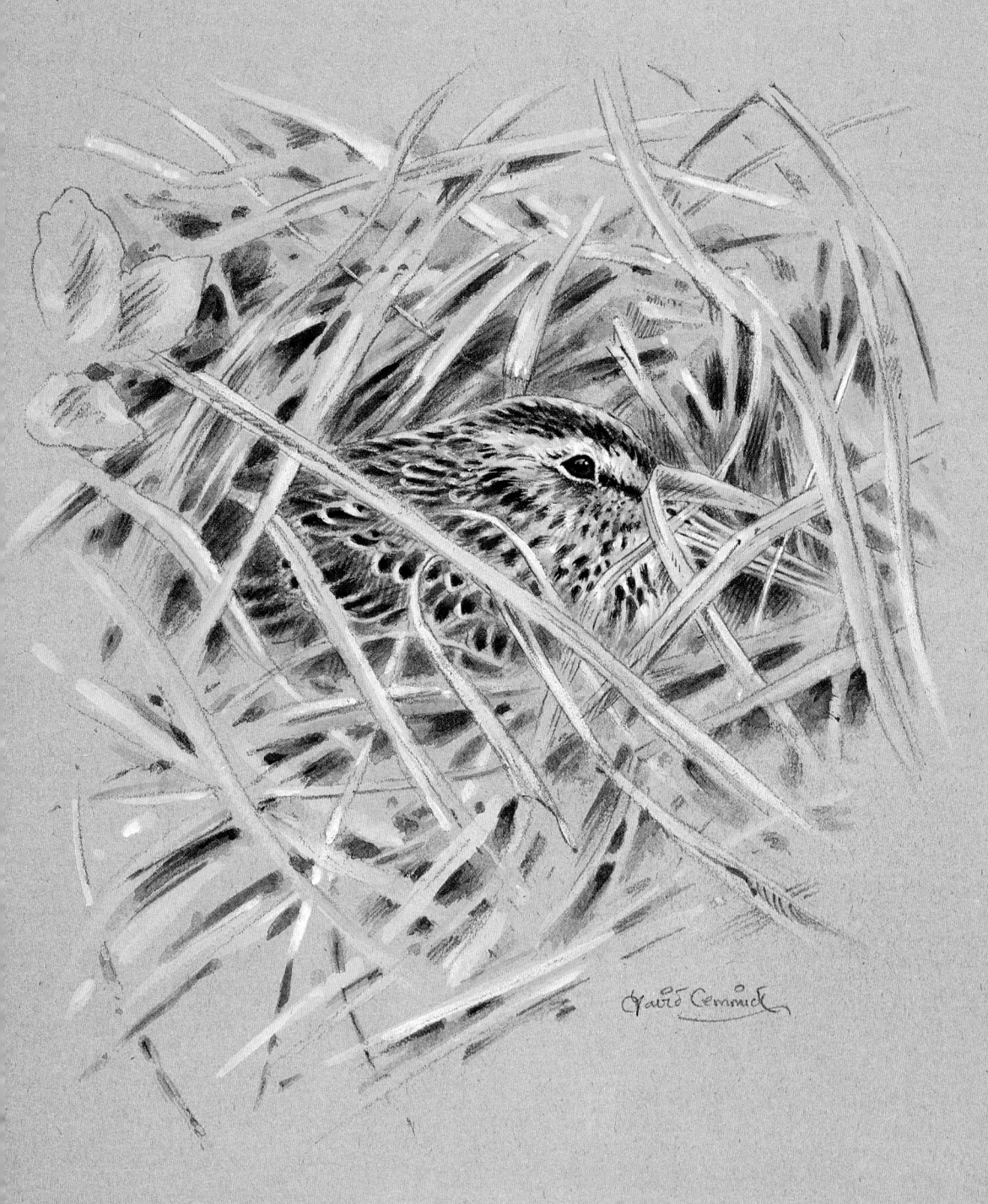

'SNIPE SITTING TIGHT'
The perfect camouflage is only betrayed
by its black shining eye.

♀

Male displaying to female.
crouched tight to the ground, wings
lowered, head held low, tail vertical,
under-tail coverts spread, making
low 'churring' sounds.

♂

Scales on middle toe - right foot.

Right foot — middle toe equal to length
of head from gape to back of skull.

legs and feet
yellow/ochre — claws pale umber.

Right foot.

4
Scapulars

8
Secondaries

10
Primaries

Adult probing for food which is
fed to the chick following
closely at its side.

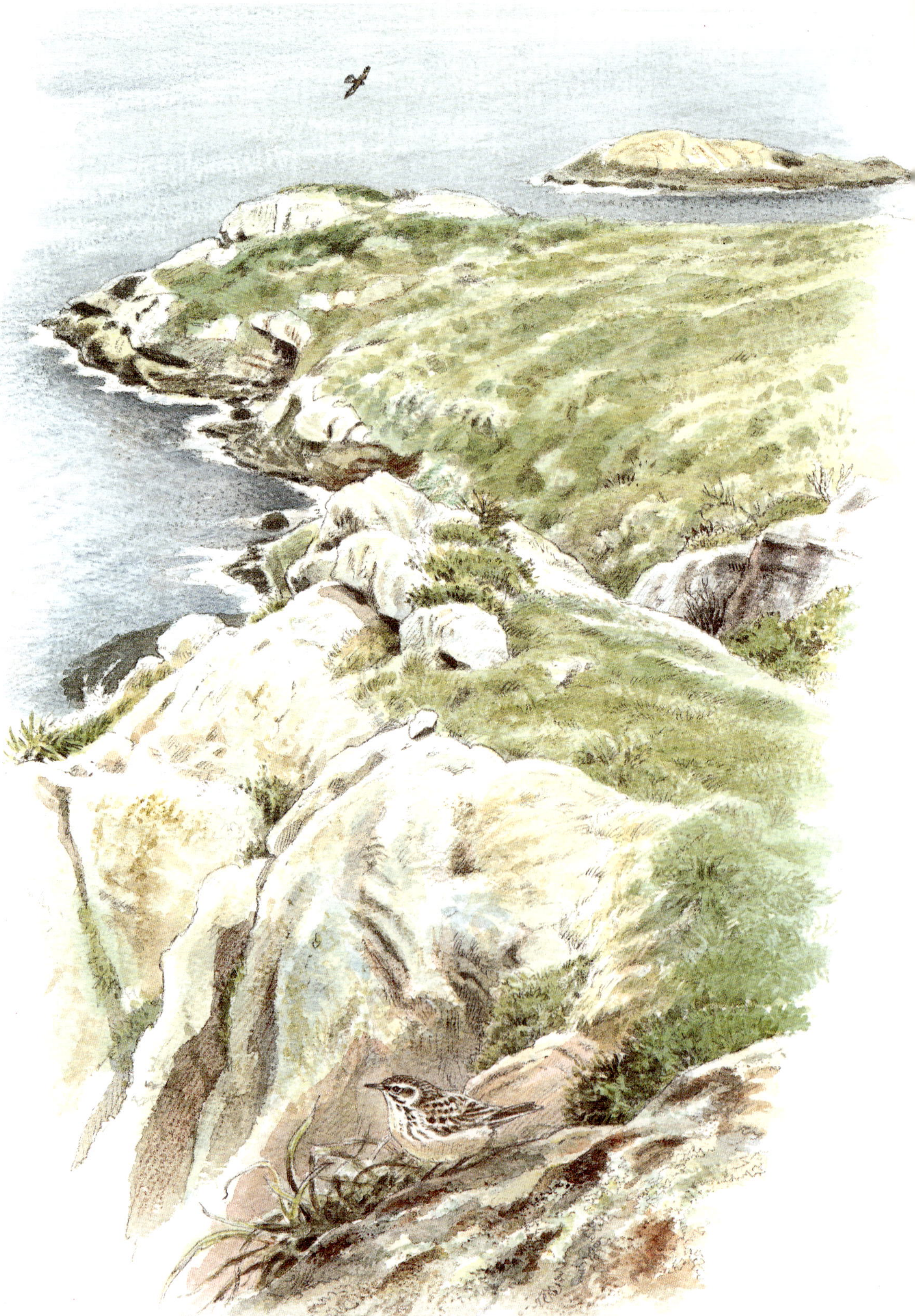

Facing page: A clear view on a very blustery day, from the hill called Rangatira, over the forest of South East Island and out to Seal Rock. In winter the seas rush up from the south and wash the top of the rock. Salt spray burns the growing tips of the vegetation recolonising the southern shores of this island that were ravaged by the agents of man more than a century ago. Gusting winds buffeted the little pipit in the foreground, as it foraged for insects high amongst the rocks.

Below: A harrier, waiting for the fog to clear.

Harrier sitting dejectedly in heavy mist unable to hunt

New Zealand Fur Seal *Arctocephalus forsteri*
Hundreds of these animals laze on the rocks on the south-east corner of South East Island while their pups play in the rock pools. The fur seal was a major food source for the Moriori but was nearly exterminated as a result of sealing by Europeans. Fur seals appear awkward on land but can move with surprising speed when danger threatens, and in the water are as agile as birds in flight.

The external ears of fur seals give them an almost dog-like appearance.

'OUT FOR THE COUNT' Fur seals resting near Seal Rock.

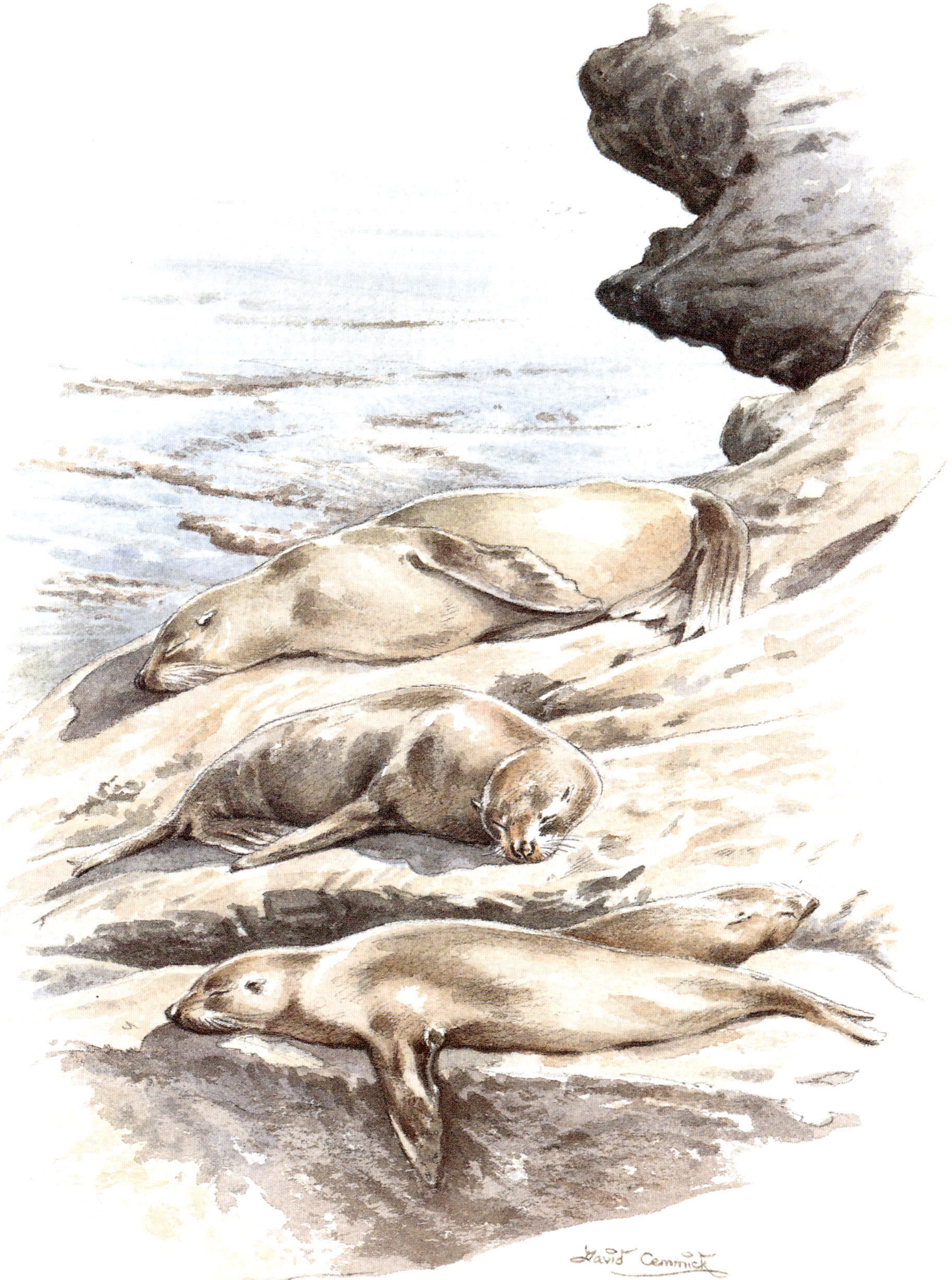

Pitt Island Shag *Stictocarbo punctatus featherstoni*
The common name of this species derives from its abundance around Pitt Island and its neighbours. Like its mainland counterpart, the spotted shag, the Pitt Island shag prefers to nest in eroded pockets or on cliff ledges. The nest is built with seaweed, or grass from a nearby clifftop, or material stolen from a neighbour. If the fishing is good some nests will have three chicks, but one or two is more common.

In the illustration below, the chick is being fed, not eaten. The chick probes deep into its parent's mouth, stimulating the regurgitation of food from the crop.

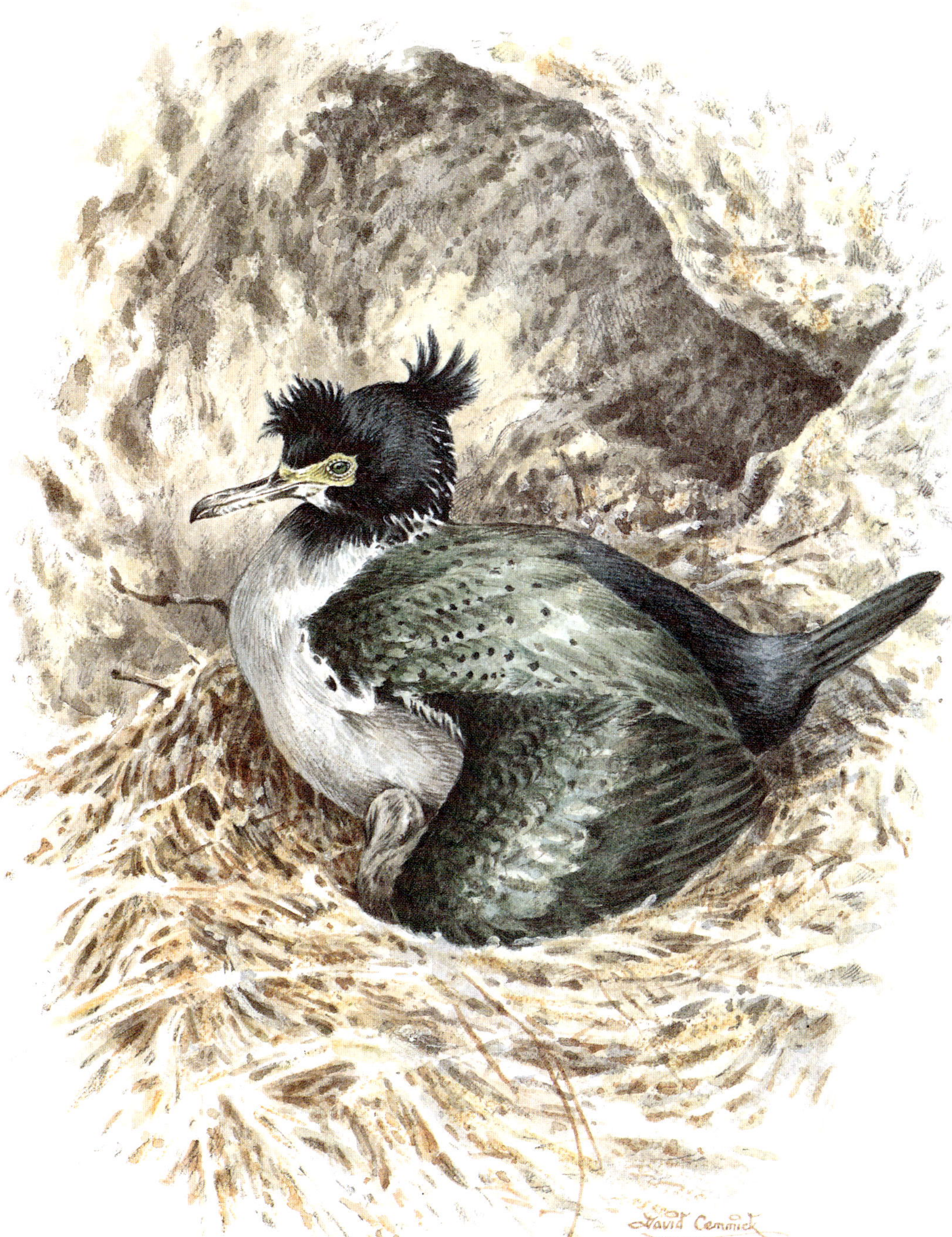
David Cemmick

The windswept rocky top of Southeast Island had a host of small and interesting things. Some plants struggle to survive while others, like this lichen growing on an Olearia shrub, turned on an unusual display of colour. From here I had a grand view across Pitt Island to the rampart tops of Mangere and Little Mangere Islands.

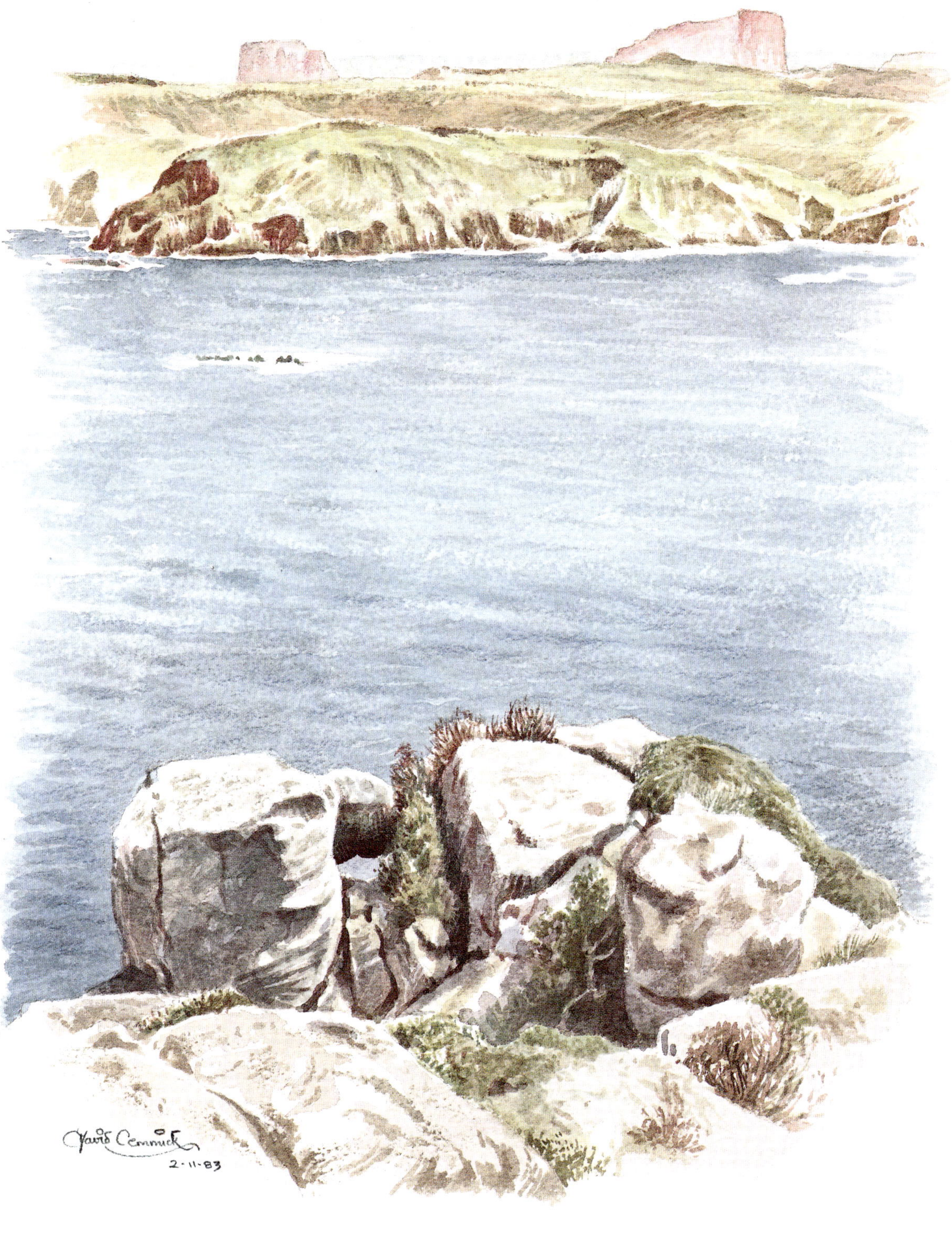
David Cemmick
2·11·83

New Zealand Shore Plover *Thinornis novaeseelandiae*
When known to the Maori in New Zealand as tuturuatu, the shore plover was widespread, but not very common, around the coasts and harbours. Its habit of nesting close to the shore in dense vegetation probably made it easy prey for predators. By 1880 it existed only on South East Island.

Attempts by the Wildlife Service to establish a second population on Mangere Island have failed: even juveniles, shifted when very young, with their wings partly clipped to reduce their powers of flight, fly back to South East Island as soon as the feathers grow. The present population on South East Island fluctuates between 100 and 140 birds.

For this painting David used a hide placed just two metres from the nest. There are usually three eggs in a clutch and the adults share incubation. The longest incubating period was 53 minutes. The male's average time on the nest was 32 minutes, and the female's, 43. On a number of occasions the male left the nest in a hurry when he could hear a territorial dispute between neighbours down on the shore.

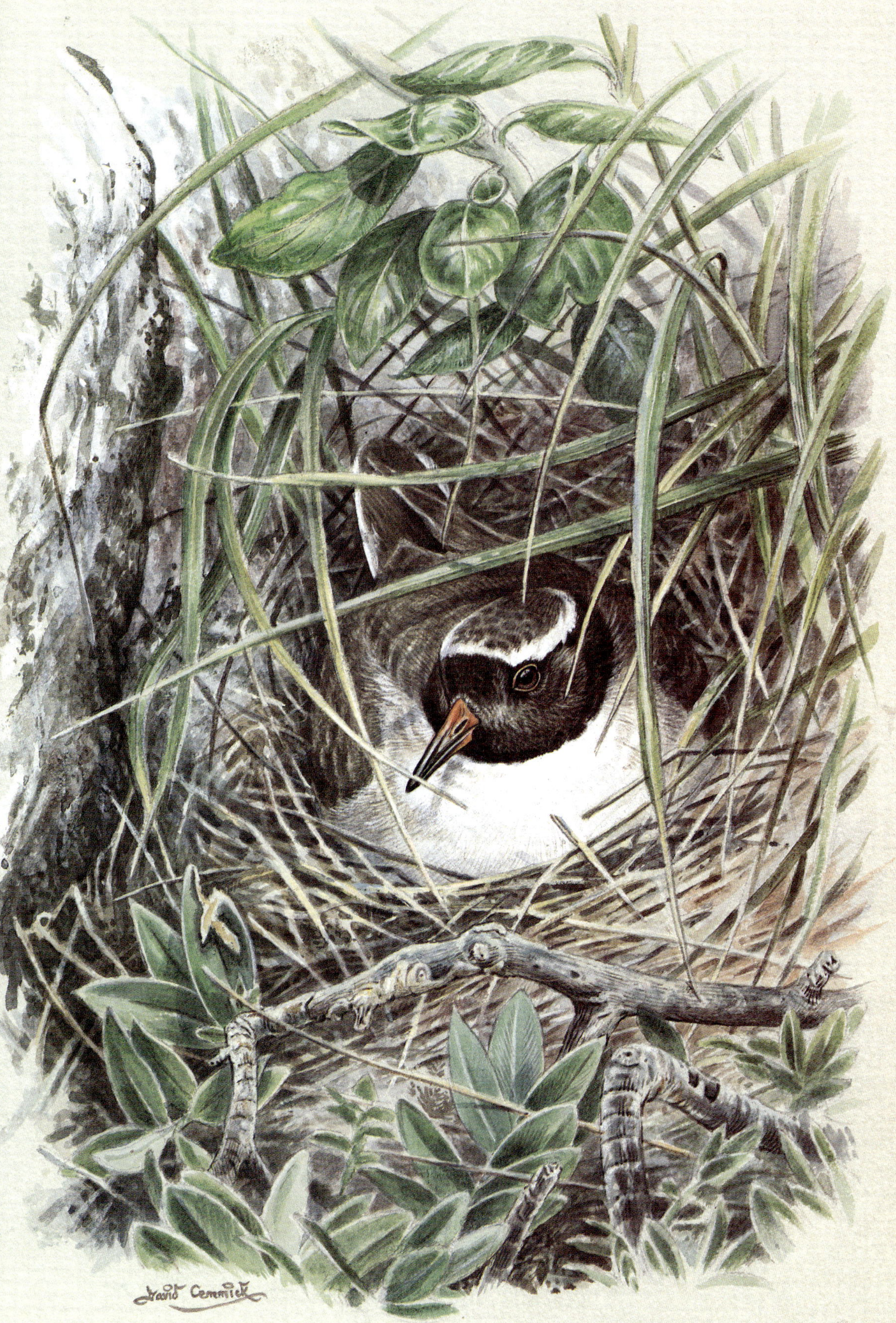
David Cemmick

Above and facing page: New Zealand shore plover.

♀

♀

Above: A giant petrel wheeling round the cliffs of Western Bay on South East Island, with the 'Pyramid', nine kilometres away, on the horizon. This rock, covered in albatrosses and mollymawks, their nests, eggs, chicks, and guano, is just as nature made it: remote, inaccessible, inhospitable. We could look at it from the shores of South East Island and be thankful that there are still some places beyond the reach of humans.

Royal Albatross

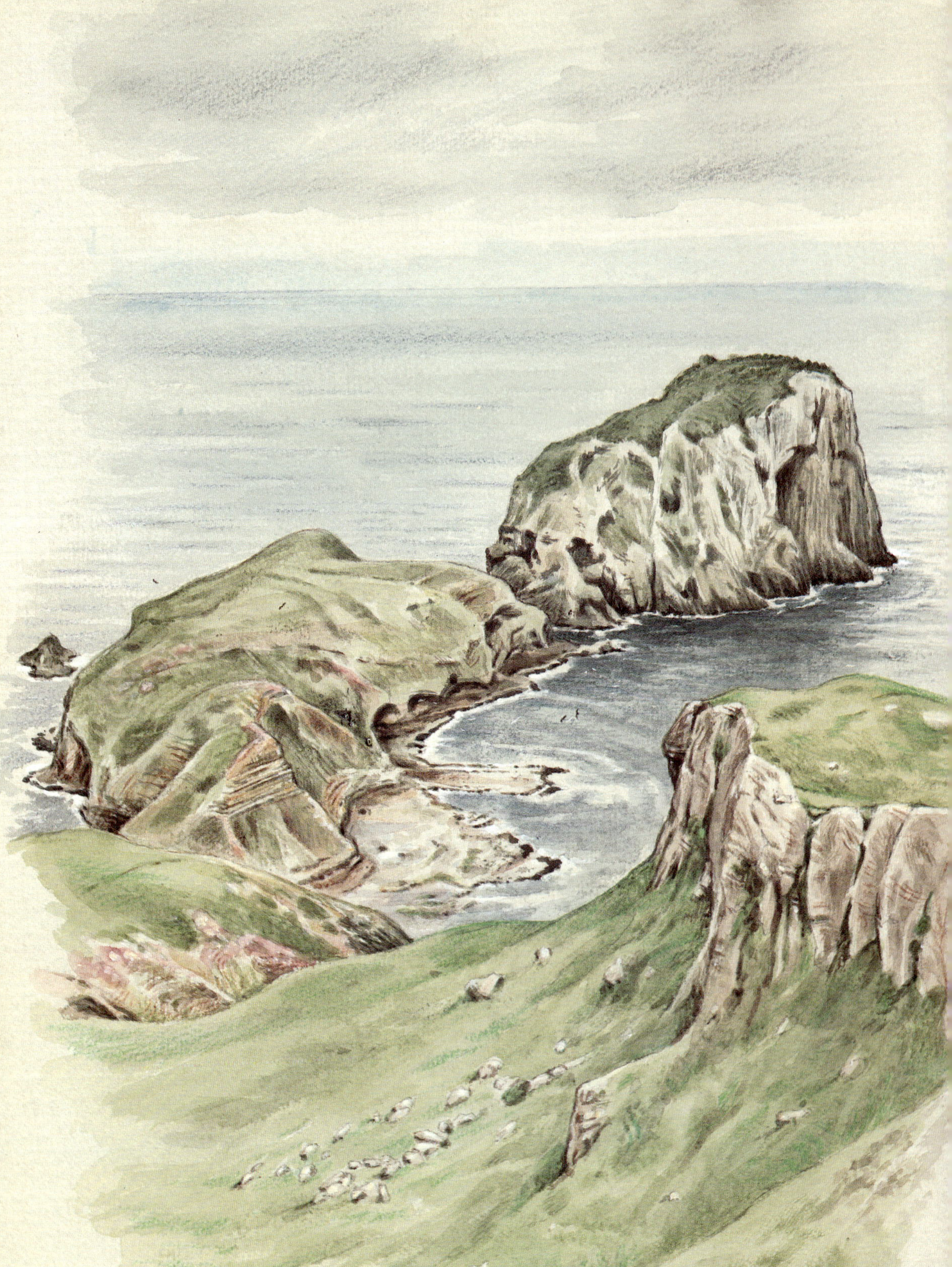
David Cemmick

Mangere Island

WE TRAVELLED TO Mangere Island from South East in John Preece's sturdy aluminium crayfishing boat. The weatherman had been predicting storm force winds but they did not eventuate, and in less than an hour we were approaching Mangere Island.

This change of workplace was arranged partly as a special treat for David, so that he could see more of the Chatham Islands, and partly because Don, who had been on Mangere for the previous month, needed a first-hand look at the work with black robins on South East Island.

From the south-east or north-west, Mangere and Little Mangere islands look like a half-submerged dumb-bell. The 'shaft' is broken at the south-east end and Little Mangere lies separated from Mangere by a narrow channel.

Little Mangere is forest capped and looks sheer-sided for most of its 180 metre height. Officially it has an area of 17 hectares, but after deducting rock and herbfield, the area of woody vegetation left is less than five hectares, and less than one hectare of this can truly be called forest.

The larger 113 hectare Mangere Island — the shaft and north-east end of the dumb-bell — has a long history of change. Farming was started toward the end of last century, and although little of the forest was felled, fire and salt-laden winds, assisted by the grazing of sheep, removed all but a tiny four hectare patch. This was saved quite accidentally because it is growing among huge boulders at the foot of the north-east cliffs which rise to 287 metres above sea level.

Goats and rabbits were also introduced late last century, but the goats must have been later removed to assist the sheep farming. To control the rabbits, cats were introduced, and they did an excellent job, for they eradicated the rabbits and then, having no winter food supply, died out themselves in the 1950s. With the removal of the bush, and the introduction of cats, however, at least fourteen kinds of bird disappeared.

Facing page: From the summit of Mangere Island, 287 metres above sea level, there is a grand view the length of the island and on to Little Mangere.

In 1966 the Royal Forest and Bird Protection Society joined with the Government to purchase Mangere Island for use as a reserve. The Wildlife Service removed the 250 sheep remaining from the 800 usually grazed, and now the island is free of introduced mammals.

Some of the forest birds, and many of the nesting seabirds, have returned. Improvement and enlargement of the remaining forest, assisted by nursery-grown trees, has been remarkable, but there is still little more than four hectares of forest. The rest of the island, where soil and weather permit, is covered in lush grass and low-growing vegetation, much of which is endemic to the Chatham Islands but now rare on the main islands.

New forest cannot grow easily through this dense sward of grass so, again with assistance from the Royal Forest and Bird Society, the Wildlife Service has planted 140,000 Chatham Island akeake trees in areas away from the old bush. Some of these are behind shelter belts of flax, some in sheltered hollows, and others on ridges to form wind breaks. All are struggling to grow in the salt-laden winds, but, in the years to come, Mangere will have a new forest.

The usual landing places on Mangere Island are on either side of the narrow south-west end — the shaft of the dumb-bell. On the south-east side there is a fine rock wharf, but the southerly swells often prevent access. On the north-west side is an extensive rock shelf at high tide level, but because of the swell kicked up by prevailing westerly winds and sea-bottom contours nearby, it is not often that boats can use this as a wharf. Fortunately there is a tiny natural harbour so we can use a dinghy with relative ease.

The old Mangere woolshed was, and the present hut is, just up the hill from this harbour. The woolshed was not very big and little sign of it remains today. The hut, in comparison with the woolshed on South East Island, was a palace: a door to keep the wind out; windows; a level floor; clean water from a tap; a loo-cum-shower; bunks with mattresses and pillows; and enough bench space for all our needs; all in a space just five metres

Mangere Hut — Luxury accommodation compared with the woodshed on southeast island.

square. To add to this the solar panel worked well here, and after dark, in this small white-painted hut, we had more than enough light — silent light.

At the same time as David and I travelled to Mangere, Don, who had been working on Mangere Island, moved to South East, taking with him another clutch of black robin eggs. Geordie stayed on South East for a few days before returning to Chatham Island to help Mike Imber search for the breeding place of the taiko. Until it was time for more robin eggs to be transferred, Nigel stayed on Mangere with us. Our regular task then was walking the length of Mangere from hut to bush to keep an eye on the cycle of black robin nesting activity. The track we took was far different from that on South East: here it is through grassland, where fence standards marked the way. And there was much to see: herbs, grasses and orchids, storm petrels burrowing, quaint insects each on their own special plants, a pipit's nest, and flax seeds sprouting.

In the bush our work was much the same as before, but this time the black robin eggs were in their rightful nests, and their parents — real black robins.

SKINK SKETCHES — *Leiolopisma nigriplantare*.

A single shining scale on the underside of each eyelid, only visible when the eyes are closed, gives the impression that the skink is watching with eyes half open, when in fact it is asleep.

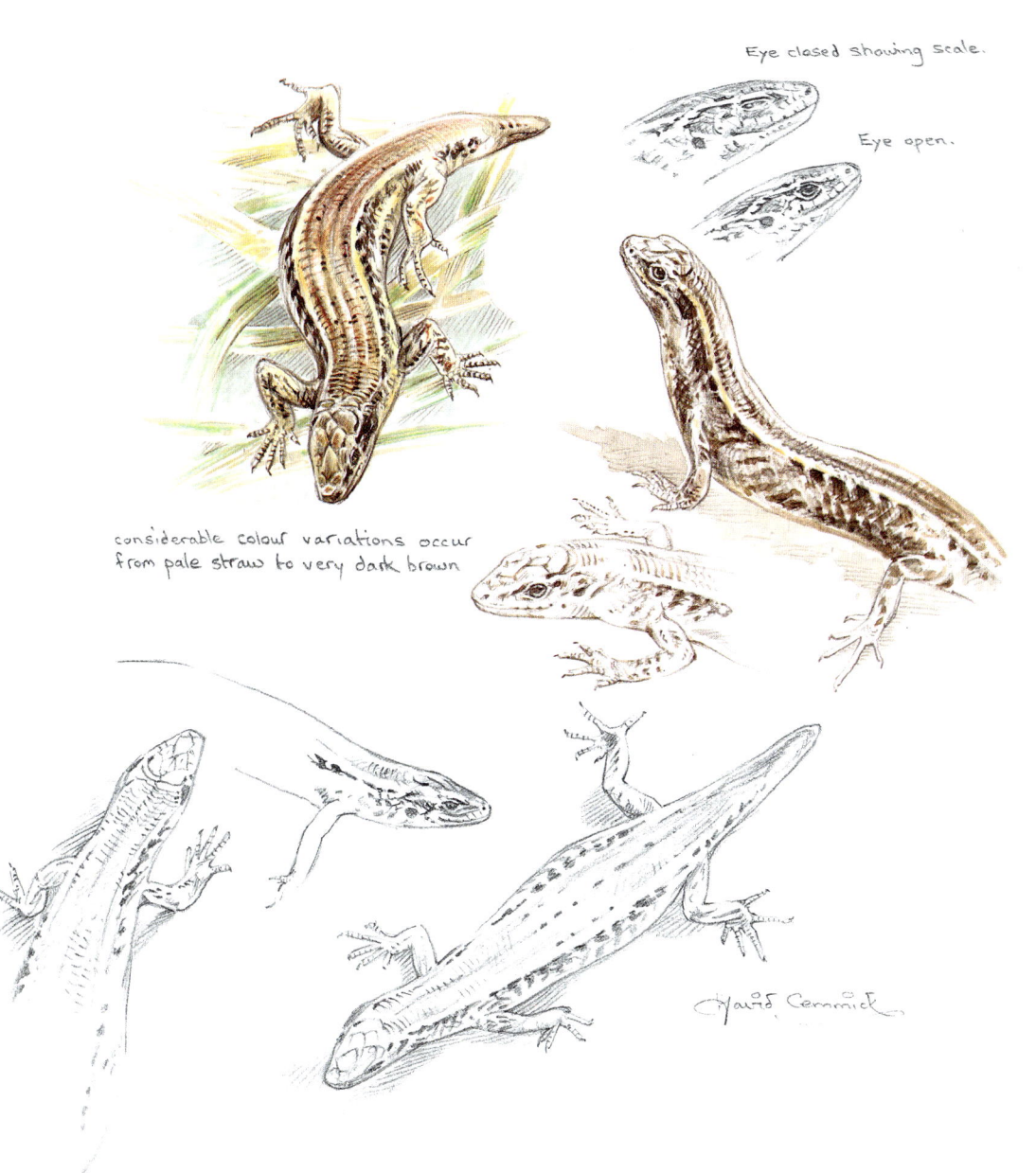

Eye closed showing scale.

Eye open.

considerable colour variations occur from pale straw to very dark brown

Chatham Island Skink *Leiolepisma nigriplantare*
The Chatham Island skink is the only lizard found on the Chatham islands but it has never been found on the main island. On a sunny day they can be seen sunbathing in sheltered places.

Chatham Island Tui *Prosthemadera novaeseelandiae chathamensis*
Unlike its extinct fellow-honeyeater, the Chatham Island bellbird, the tui is found wherever suitable habitats exist, and flies considerable distances to feed in new habitats, such as the flax plantings on Mangere Island. Although found on all the Chatham islands, it is plentiful only on South East Island. Its song may be described as an abbreviation of that of the mainland tui.

pollen on forehead from feeding on flax.

wings closed in descent.

HEAD, CHEST & BELLY BOTTLE GREEN. UPPER FLANK VIOLET SHEEN. DARK CHESTNUT BACK. SECONDARIES TURQUOISE SHEEN. PRIMARIES GREEN. (including coverts) UPPER TAIL COVERTS GREEN & BLUE. LEGS & FEET GREY. PINK UNDER TOES.

territorial threat display.

Tui feeding on flax.

David Cemmick

101

Chatham Island Oystercatcher *Haematopus chathamensis*
This short-legged member of the worldwide oystercatcher genus is a bird of the rocky shores. It is still found throughout its natural range, over all the Chatham islands, but only on South East Island is it really thriving. The total population is less than 200 birds.

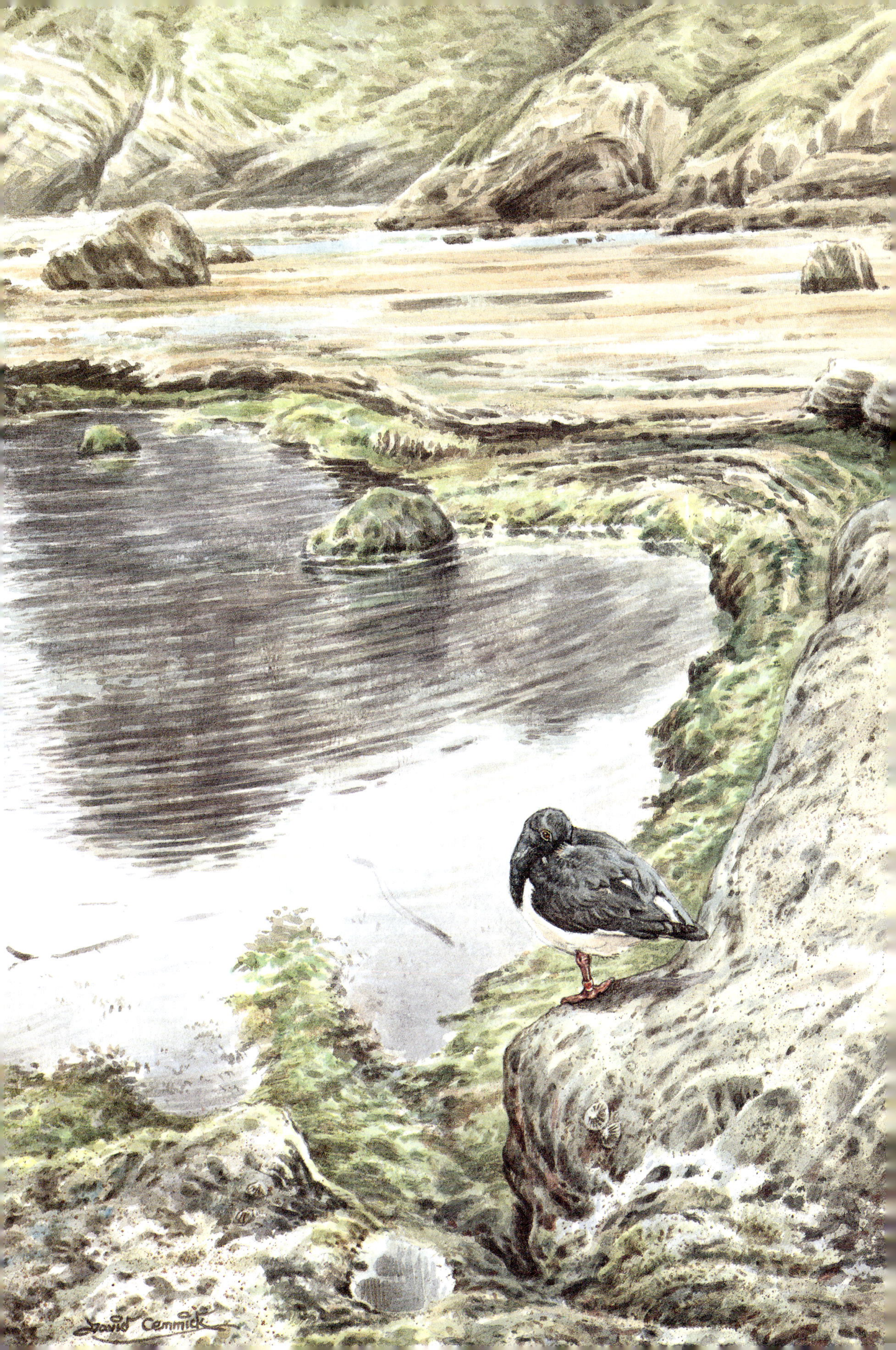
David Cemmick

Female: Shorter bill with squarer end not as brightly coloured as male. More angular, domed head than male. Distinct grooving around nostrils. Rounder chest.
Male. Bright, tapering pointed bill. Irregular pupil.

104

Very knobbly, fleshy feet pinkish/ochre.
ochre nails with naples pads and heels.

105

Chatham Island Blue Penguin *Eudyptula minor chathamensis*
To the casual observer the Chatham Island blue penguin looks like the mainland species, but its habits have been modified a little to suit local conditions.

In the evening and early night groups of six to twelve penguins gather at the water's edge before climbing ashore and hurrying (as much as any penguin can hurry) over the open, skua-patrolled rock platform to the safety of the bush. Some nest burrows are close to the bush edge, but others may be hundreds of metres inland or nearly at the top of the hill. It seems to take them hours to get up there but the downward trip can be a speedy toboggan on a well-rounded tummy.

After the eggs are laid, incubation and feeding of the chicks by both parents takes more than three months.

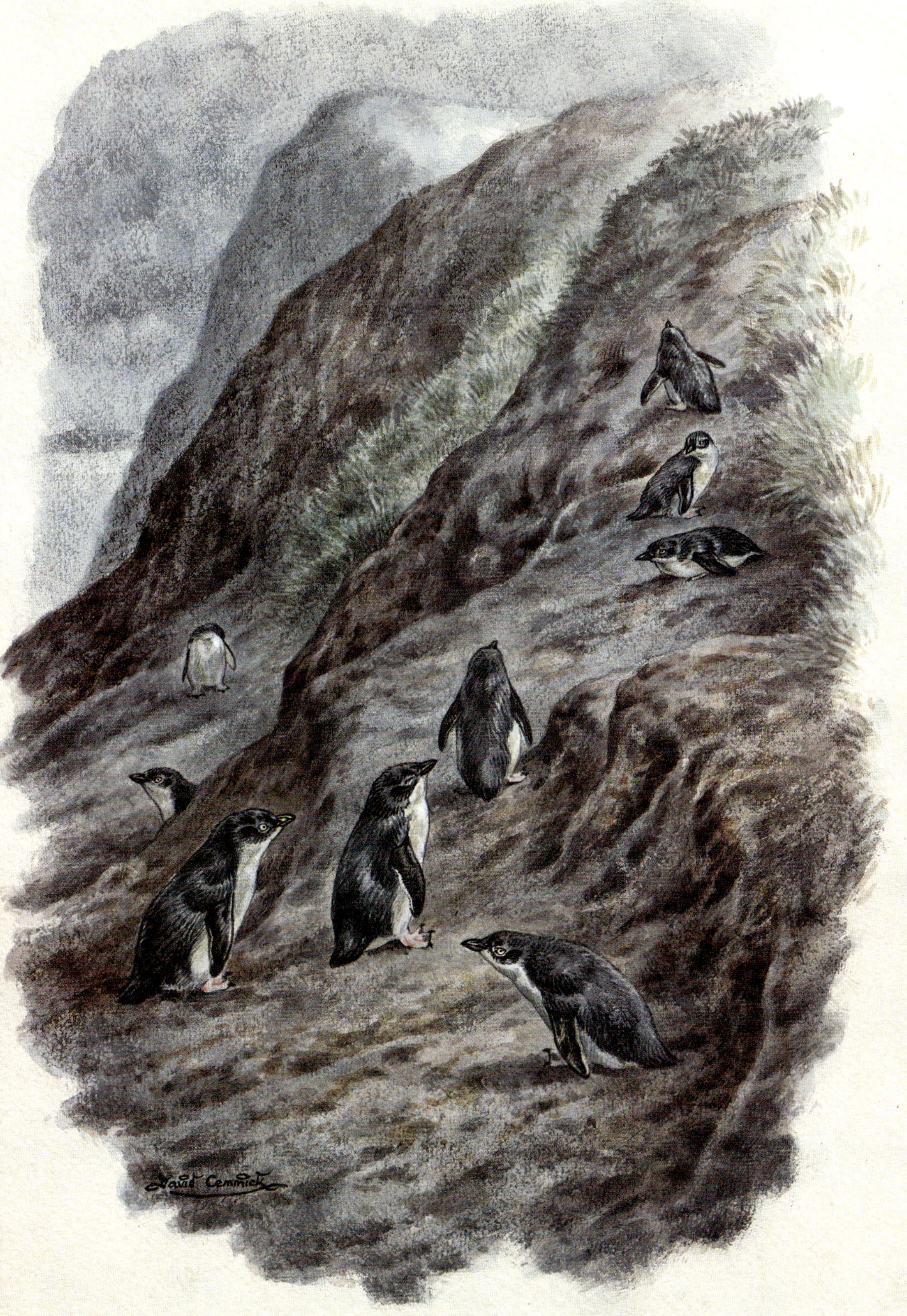

apprehensive stance

During copulation the male drums its flippers vigorously against the sides of its mate

CHATHAM ISLAND
BLUE PENGUIN
Mangere Island — 27th Nov 1983

'tobogganing'

A flashlight strapped to my forehead left my hands free for sketching, some inquisitive birds coming within inches of me as I worked.
Drawn between 11.30 p.m - 12.30 p.m 27·11·83.

Below: This Spider, like many insects on remote islands, may not have a name. Indeed, predator-free islands are just as much a haven for insects as they are for birds. Rats in particular would relish a meal of this size: five centimetres from head to tail. Remote islands are rarely visited by entomologists, who regard them as safe places best kept for another day, while they study the many thousands of mainland species, some of which are in threatened habitats and others diminishing in number.

Facing page: The summit of Mangere Island and the steep slopes down to the bush — home to a quarter of the black robin population. How easy it would be for one large rock-fall to destroy them.

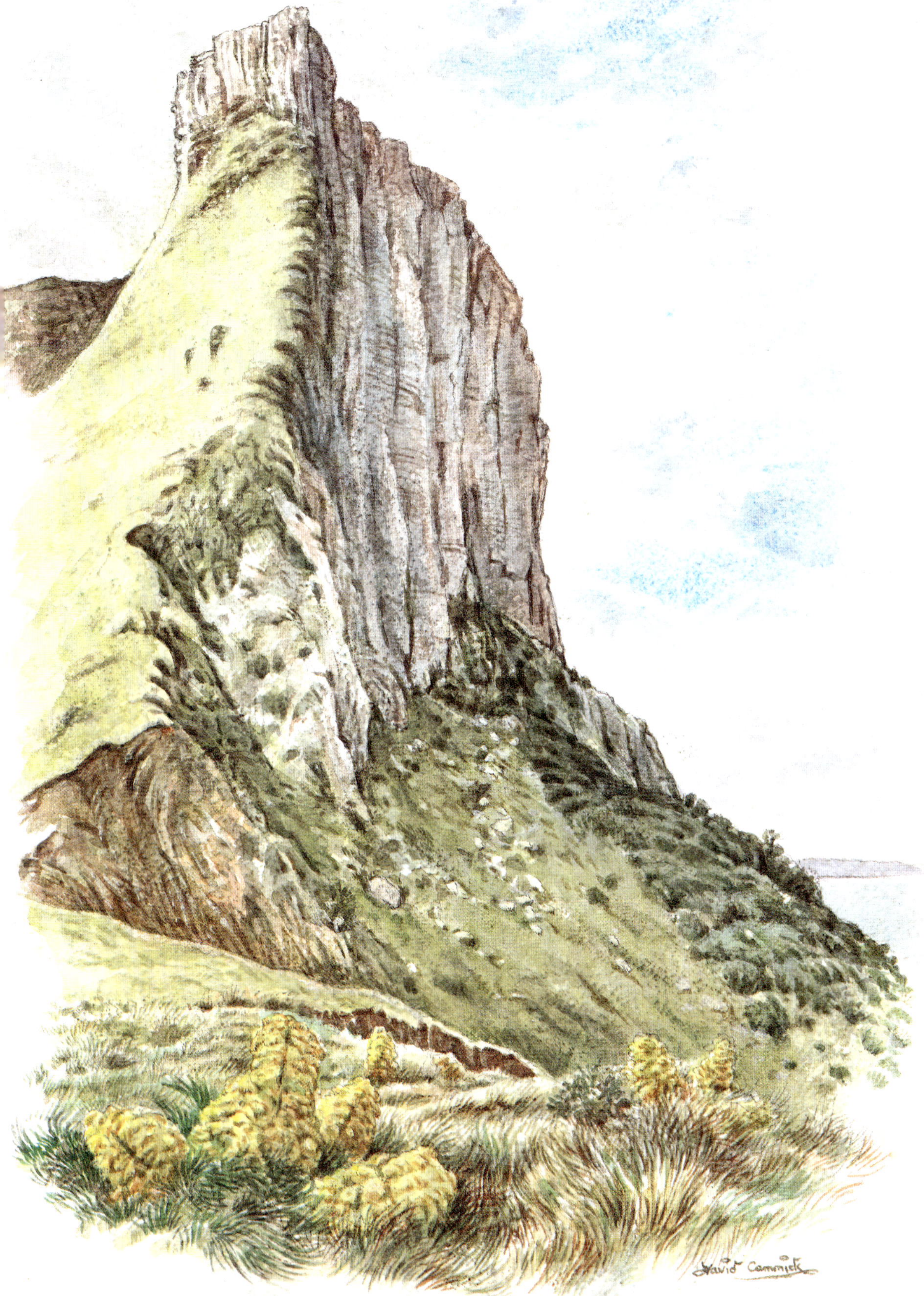
David Cammick

A Growing Population

THE SPRING OF 1981 began with three pairs of black robins and one single male. Two pairs reared no young in that year but trusty old Blue and her mate went to work with vigour. She was allowed to incubate her first clutch for a while, then one egg was put in a warbler's nest on Mangere Island and the other taken to a tit's nest on South East Island. Both hatched. The tits proved to be excellent parents so the chick from the warbler's nest was taken when it was seven days old — still almost naked and with its eyes barely open — to South East to join its sibling.

Meanwhile Blue had laid again and both her eggs had been taken to a tit's nest on South East. Only one of these hatched. By Christmas there were three healthy young robins on South East, but these young birds could not stay there — they had to spend time near their rightful parents. Back to Mangere they went, shortly before Blue raised two more chicks without human help. Thus, in the 1981/82 summer five chicks were raised bringing the total population to twelve.

Later in the year two birds died and the 1982 season began with four pairs and two single females. Sadly it was a bad summer for many birds and only a single black robin chick was reared.

By now it was obvious that the little bit of forest on Mangere was too small for four pairs of productive robins. In January 1983 one pair was moved to South East Island. They did well, so a further pair was shifted, but for more than the next six months, they could not be found. Then the female alone was seen. The male must have died. This left two pairs and two single females on Mangere and one pair and a single female on South East to start the 1983 season. With us to help them, and a better knowledge of now proven cross-fostering techniques, we all had high hopes.

All the thinking, scheming, match-making, nest manipulation, experimentation, and cross-fostering was planned by Don Merton. Cross-fostering, as a management technique, has been used before in captivity, or to take eggs from wild birds into captivity. The black robin project is

David Cemmick

the first time cross-fostering has been used in the management of an endangered songbird living in the wild. The experience does not stop there, for the technique, with modifications, is now being used in the black stilt and the takahe management programmes.

Modification and innovation are probably the keynotes of such operations. The incubators and transfer boxes we now use are the result of many years' experimentation, but the container Don used to transfer that first live black robin chick from Mangere to South East was the height of innovation. He lined a stout wooden box with polystyrene and placed a heated can of corned beef in the bottom as a 'hot water bottle'. On top of that sat a milk powder tin, with holes for ventilation, containing a second-hand robin nest as a genuine bed for the chick during its two-hour sea passage. The box was then made dark inside so that the chick would sleep rather than use up energy begging for food, and the whole device was tested by carrying a warbler chick around Mangere Island for a few hours.

With all this experience to draw on, Don's plan for the 1983 season was to let the robins incubate their first clutches for a week or so, then put all the eggs into tit nests on South East Island. Then we would take all the second clutch eggs as soon as they were laid and put them into tit nests. Third clutches we would leave with the robins and all their young would stay on the islands where they were raised. And that, more or less, is just how it happened.

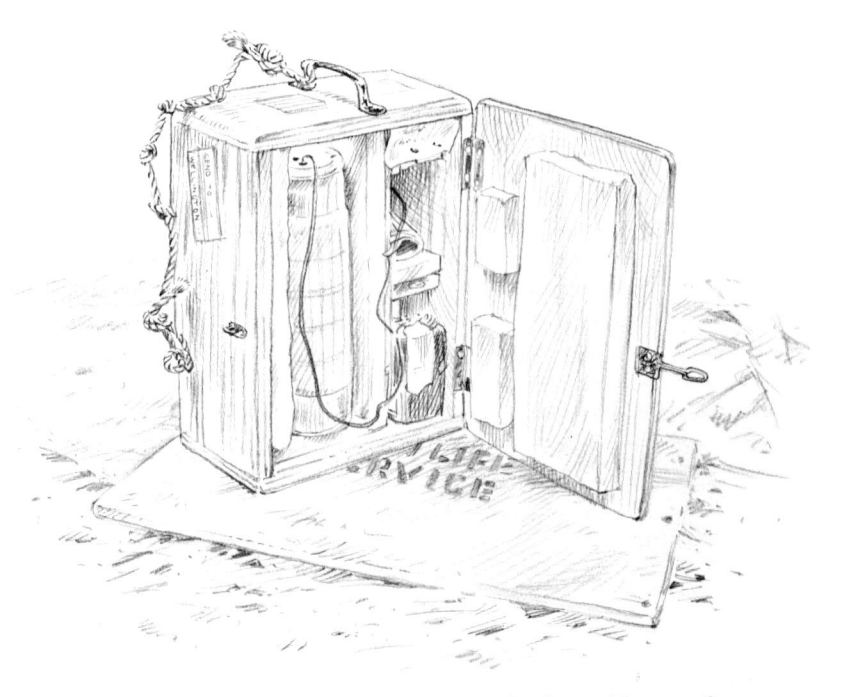

Above: The incubator specially designed and built for transferring robin eggs from island to island.

The complicated pair swapping, match-making, egg and chick transfers are illustrated here in Don's chart (stolen from the Mangere hut wall) which hides some curious events. Young Green laid three clutches of three eggs, and Ngaio (A-R), the female on South East Island, had a third clutch, also with three eggs. Previously, all black robin clutches had been two eggs. One tit nest with two robin eggs was wrecked by a seabird in the night. Don carefully cleaned the one remaining cold but whole egg and placed it in another tit nest; it hatched. One of the male robins on Mangere Island decided, after his mate had hatched two chicks, that the spare female next door was more attractive. As a female alone cannot raise two chicks Don became 'Uncle' for a few weeks. So, for the 1983 season, three pairs of black robins produced a total of 22 eggs; 17 of these hatched, 13 fledged, 11 reached independence, and by the end of the summer there were 20 black robins.

During this, our 1983, visit, 'Old Blue', one of the females who was at least 13 years old, was still alive. I use the term 'at least' because she was an adult when first given her blue colour band — she could have been 14 years or older. As the oldest survivor of the original transfer she saw a unique course of events which we all hope will result in the survival of the species.

115

Chatham Island Yellow-Crowned Parakeet
Cyanoramphus auriceps forbesi
A few years ago the total population of the yellow-crowned parakeet was counted to be 18 birds on Mangere and Little Mangere islands. Its forest habitat had diminished and deteriorated, and red-crowned parakeets were taking over. Now that the forest is improving and we are working to keep the red-crowns out, yellow-crowned parakeet numbers have increased. The few observation reports we have suggest that the yellow-crowns do not produce as many young as the red-crowns. They, like all our parakeets, prefer to nest in deep holes in trees, so it is hard to see what happens in the nest. The old *Olearia traversi* trees in the boulder-strewn Mangere forest have an abundance of nest sites for parakeets.

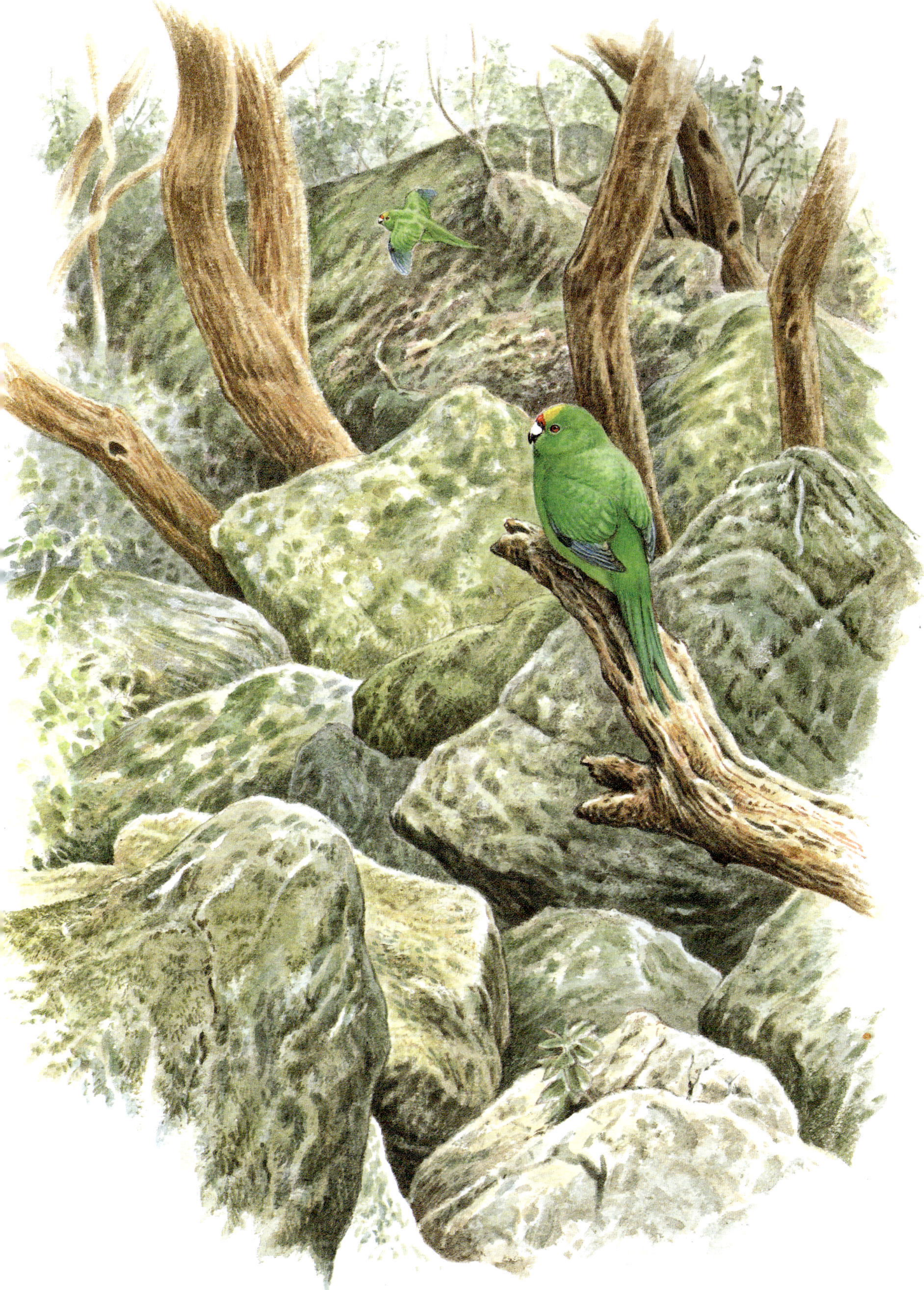

Yellow Crowned or Forbes Parakeet -

Occasionally interbreeding occurs between Red and Yellow Crowned parakeets. The hybrid offspring can be recognized by red feathering on the ear coverts.

Fairy Prion *Pachyptila turtur*
We did not see many fairy prions during our visit. Usually, we saw them at night as they returned to their nest burrows, and only occasionally could we see large flocks well out to sea. One afternoon an onshore wind brought many hundreds close to shore, the dark inverted 'W' across the wings being a useful identification of the prion group.

Fairy prion headstudies and bill detail.

Fairy prions at sea – the stark silhouette of Sail Rock against the western horizon as seen from Mangere Island.

Southern Great Skua *Stercorarius skua lonnbergi*
In winter the skuas are the scavengers of the sea; in summer, harvesters of slow petrels. They seem ungainly on land but, in fact, they catch most of their prey by hunting for prions and petrels in the forest at night. There is no doubt that they are the avian lords of these petrel islands. Here, unlike other places where they have been studied, the adult birds are frequently in trios. There is no sure way to distinguish the sexes of these birds, but observations suggest that most trios comprise two males and one female.

Each trio or pair owns a territory, usually a rocky promontory or area of short coastal vegetation, where a nest of grasses and leaves is built and usually two eggs laid. If a trio is present then all birds assist with incubation and feeding the young. Feeding themselves on small prey is no problem as it can be swallowed whole and the undigested bits regurgitated later, but to eat a larger item, or feed bits to a chick, needs the assistance of a mate so that they can have a 'tug-of-war' to tear the food apart.

Little is known about the arguments involved in a pair or trio becoming established after their winter at sea. Nor have the 'discussions' between a pair or trio and their neighbours in the course of establishing a territory been closely studied. But, once territory has been established, the raising of wings or 'heraldic display', as shown opposite, is a clear message of ownership to approaching birds.

'A Skua pellet.'
This was once a Storm Petrel.

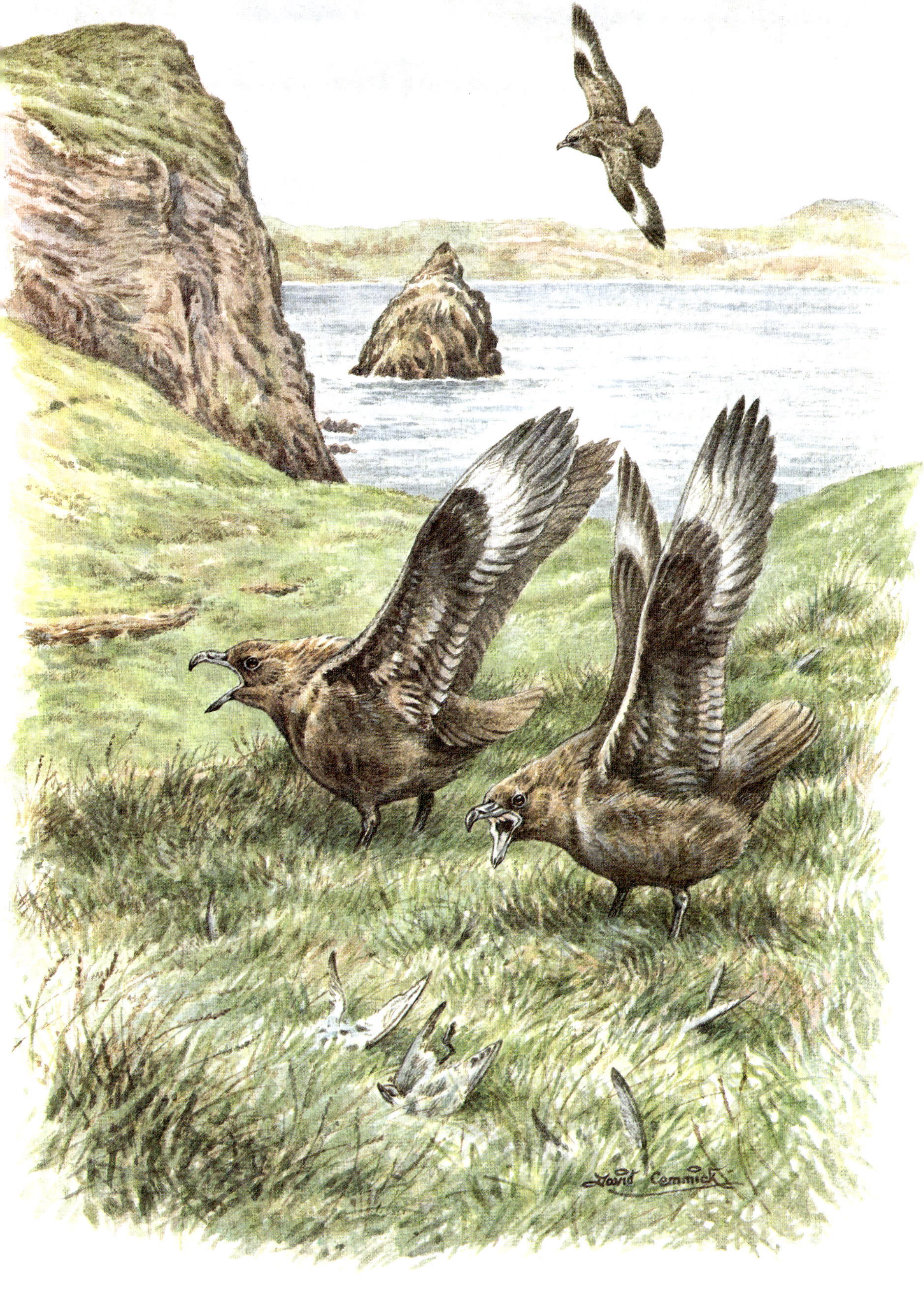
David Cemmick

SKUA CHICK — Mangere Island 25 Nov 83.

'HERALDIC' territorial Skua display.

Head up - wings back
Head down - wing verticle.

'stiff wing' display.

125

The huge elastic gape of a skua enables it to swallow smaller prey species in one piece, the indigestable matter being regurgitated as a neat pellet.

Below: Macabre remains from night-time sorties of skuas whose coastal territories were littered with blue penguin carcases such as this and those of other seabirds.

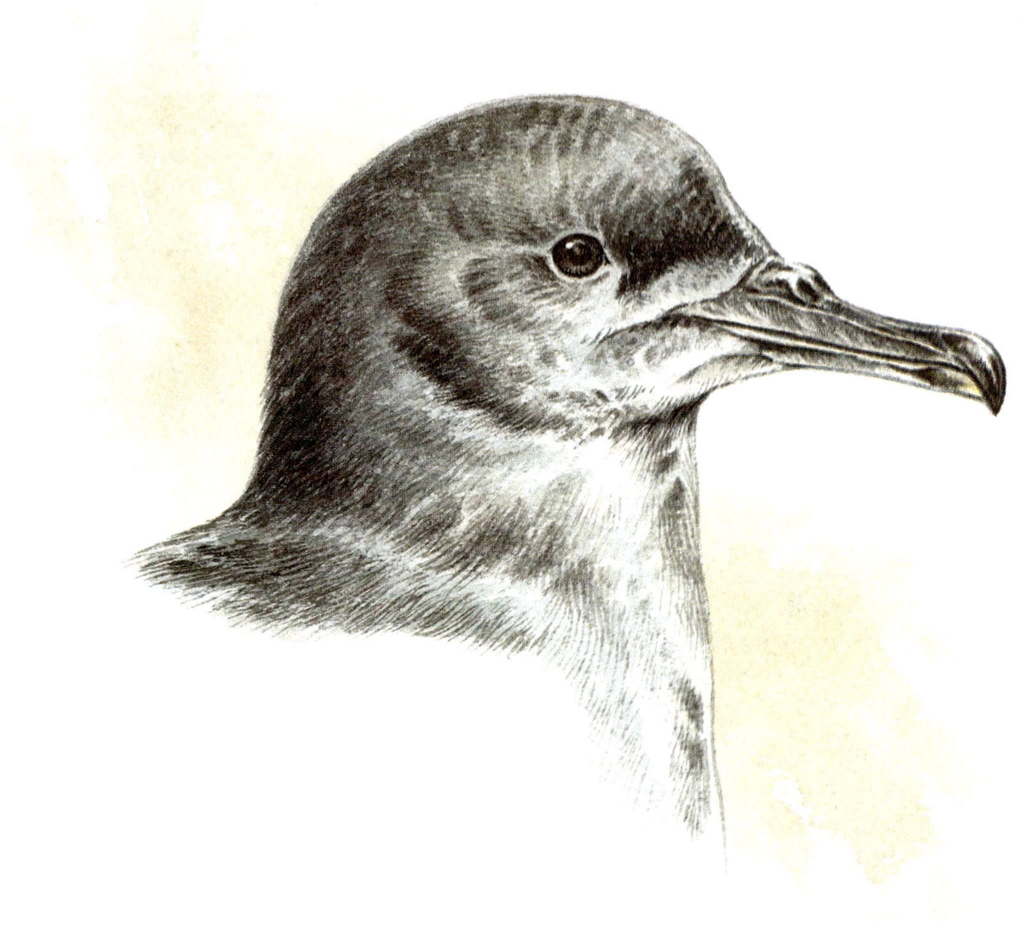
David Cemmick

Sooty Shearwater *Puffinus griseus*
There are some shearwaters on South East Island and some on Mangere, but to see the thousands — or tens of thousands — returning to Little Mangere at dusk, is one of the seabird spectaculars. Equally striking is the sight of the birds shoulder to shoulder, in the early morning darkness, shuffling toward a take-off point.

Sooty shearwaters, which also breed on the islands around Stewart Island, Snares, Campbell, Auckland, and other subantarctic islands, and on islands off the coast of Chile, are one of our long-distance migrants, spending the southern winter near Alaska, and returning southward only to breed. It is the young of this species that the Maori gather as muttonbirds from the islands around Stewart Island.

Sooty shearwaters sketched by flashlight whilst returning to their burrows on Mangere

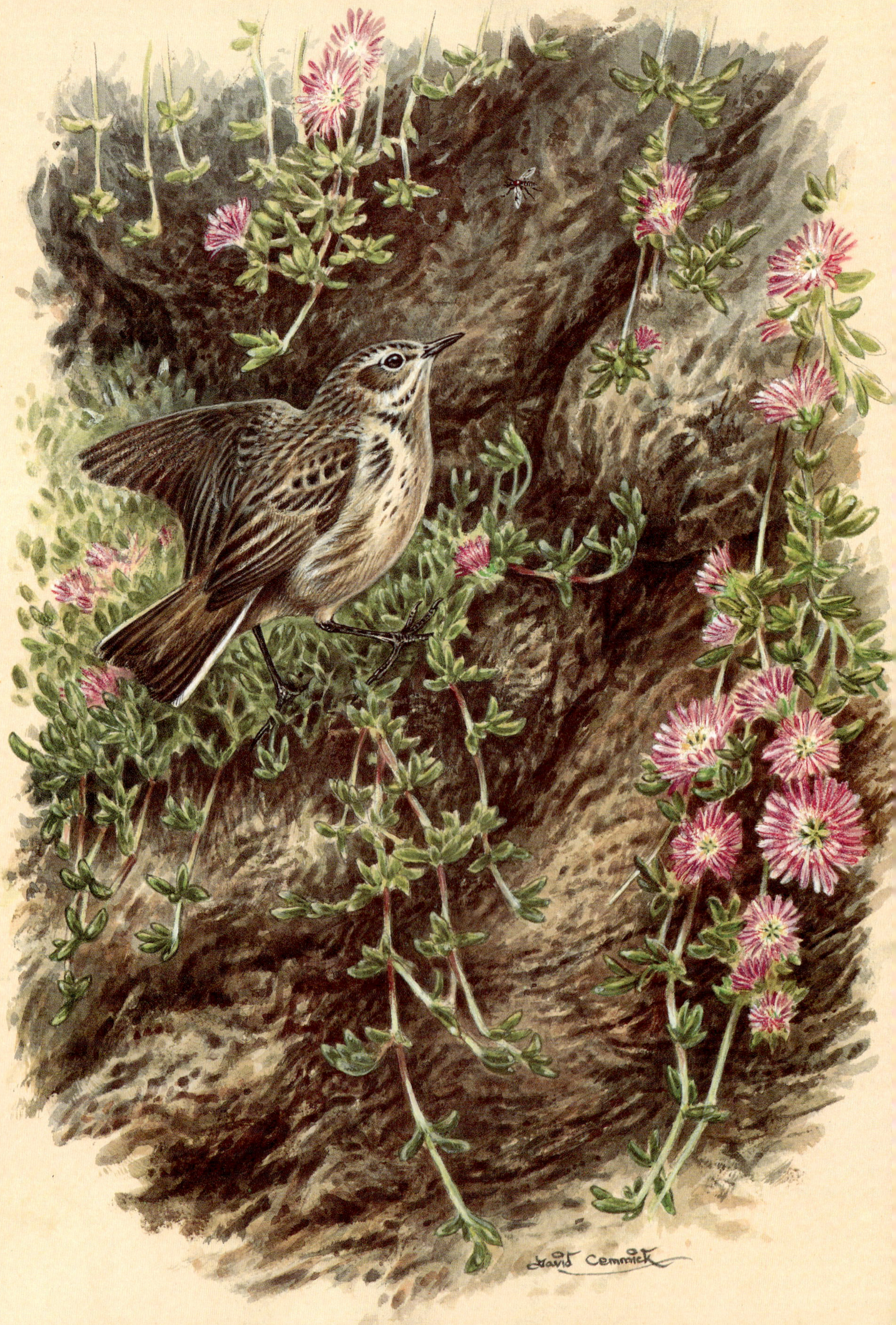
David Cemmick

New Zealand Pipit *Anthus novaeseelandiae novaeseelandiae*
This bird of the coasts and rough grassland of many parts of New Zealand is one of the few species to benefit from man's modification of the Chatham Islands, but on South East and Mangere islands the regrowth of the forest will slowly push them back to their original coastal habitat.

The Next Year, the Year After …

IN THE SPRING of 1984 Don, Nog, Geordie, Nigel, and a few others, returned to Mangere and South East. Miraculously 19 of the 20 black robins had survived the winter. Old Blue had died after more than 13 great years. She was mother, grandmother, or great grandmother of 17 of the surviving robins.

A large proportion of the black robin population starting the 1984 season were young birds and we cannot really expect much breeding activity until these birds are two years old. However, the team of workers set out with the same sort of plan as the previous season; the older robins produced eggs as before, and a few young ones helped so that by the end of the season 31 eggs had been laid, 19 chicks reared to independence and the population totalled 38.

There are now far more robins than we have known since they were all colour banded in 1972. Some will die, but most should live, and, with the continuing help of Don and his assistants, the black robin population is climbing rapidly, away from the danger of extinction.

It is not for me to predict the future. Right now, owing to hard work by many people, and kind actions from a lot more, there are two islands in the Chatham group which have forest, are free of predators, and are safe homes for endangered birds. South East Island is large and its varied habitats are improving. Mangere is smaller, as is its forest area, and the new, man-made forest needs more help yet. Both these islands are still fragile remnants but there are no others. Their conservation has improved the lot of six rare and endangered birds, but fire, disease, or the wreck of a ship with a rat on it, could undo the work of the past 20 years. There are still bird species which are declining in number and others which live only on one island.

More mainland forest areas are being fenced and these will provide habitats for the hardier birds, but without the removal of predators, there is no way that the black robin, and some of the other endangered species, will ever return to the main Chatham island.

The Wildlife Service, and other conservation agencies, assisted by a host of generous people, will continue to work to maintain and improve these fragile island sanctuaries and others throughout New Zealand — sad remnants of a paradise lost. Lost to the rats, cats and greed of man.

The Chatham Island situation shows us that there is room for both humans and animals — even if neither think that they have enough — and, with care, we can ensure that the wildlife of today will still be there tomorrow.

Olearia flowers

Appendix: Chatham Island Birds

I. Extinct Chatham Island Birds

Extinctions Prior to European Settlement

Crested penguin   *Eudyptes* sp.*
Sooty albatross   *Phoebetria* sp.*
Mottled petrel   *Pterodroma inexpectata*†
One medium-large petrel
A large petrel   *Procellaria* sp.*
A smaller petrel thought to be the grey petrel *P. cinerea*†
Possibly Buller's shearwater   *Puffinus bulleri*†
Fluttering or Hutton's shearwater   *P. gavia*† or *P. huttoni*†
Shag   *Phalacrocorax* sp.* — smaller than other N.Z. species
New Zealand swan   *Cygnus sumnerensis**
Chatham Island duck   *Pachyanus chathamica*
New Zealand scaup   *Aythya novaeseelandiae*†

Merganser   *Mergus* sp.
Chatham Island fish eagle   *Haliaeetus* n. sp.
Little weka   *Gallirallus minor**
Weka   *G. australis*†
Giant Chatham Island rail   *Diaphorapteryx hawkinsi*
New Zealand coot   *Nesophalaris chathamensis*
Black-fronted tern   *Sterna albostriata*†
Fairy tern   *S. nereis*†
Chatham Island snipe   *Coenocorypha chathamica**
Kaka   *Nestor meridionalis*†
Laughing owl   *Sceloglaux albifacies*
New Zealand crow   *Palaeocorax moriorum*

Extinctions Subsequent to the Start of European Settlement

Australasian bittern   *Botaurus stellaris poiciloptilus*‡
Paradise shelduck   *Tadorna variegata*†
Brown teal   *Anas aucklandica chlorotis*‡
New Zealand shoveler   *A. rhynchotis variegata*‡. Last record 1925
New Zealand falcon   *Falco novaeseelandiae*†. Present in 1890s

Dieffenbach's rail   *Rallus philippensis dieffenbachi*†. Last record 1840
Chatham Island rail   *R. modestus**
Chatham Island fernbird   *Bowdleria punctata rufescens*†
Chatham Island bellbird   *Anthornis melanura melanocephala*†

II. Extant Chatham Island Birds

Endemic Species

Chatham Island taiko   *Pterodroma magentae*§
Chatham Island petrel   *P. axillaris*§
Chatham Island oystercatcher   *Haematopus chathamensis*§

Chatham Island warbler   *Gerygone albofrontata*
Black robin   *Petroica (Miro) traversi*§

Endemic Subspecies

Chatham Island blue penguin   *Eudyptula minor chathamensis*
Chatham Island mollymawk   *Diomedea cauta eremita*
Chatham fulmar prion *Pachyptila crassirostris pyramidalis*
Chatham Island shag   *Leucocarbo carunculatus onslowi*
Pitt Island shag   *Stictocarbo punctatus featherstoni*
Chatham Island snipe   *Coenocorypha aucklandica pusilla*§

Chatham Island pigeon   *Hemiphaga novaeseelandiae chathamensis*§
Chatham Island red-crowned parakeet *Cyanoramphus novaezelandiae chathamensis*
Chatham Island yellow-crowned parakeet *C. auriceps forbesi*§
Chatham Island fantail   *Rhipidura fuliginosa penitus*
Chatham Island tit   *Petroica macrocephala chathamensis*§
Chatham Island tui   *Prosthemadera novaeseelandiae chathamensis*§

* Genus extant elsewhere in New Zealand.
† Species extant elsewhere in New Zealand.
‡ Subspecies extant elsewhere in New Zealand.
§ A species that is rare or endangered.

Indigenous Species

Northern royal albatross *Diomedea epomophora sanfordi*
Buller's mollymawk *D. bulleri*
Northern giant petrel *Macronectes halli*
Black-winged petrel *Pterodroma nigripennis*
Broad-billed prion *Pachyptila vittata vittata*
Fairy prion *P. turtur*
Sooty shearwater *Puffinus griseus*
Subantarctic little shearwater *P. assimilis elegans*
Grey-backed storm petrel *Garrodia nereis*
White-faced storm petrel *Pelagodroma marina maoriana*
Southern diving petrel *Pelecanoides urinatrix chathamensis*
Black shag *Phalacrocorax carbo novaehollandiae*
Grey duck *Anas superciliosa superciliosa*
Fiji harrier *Circus approximans approximans*
Marsh crake *Porzana pusilla affinis*
Spotless crake *P. tabuensis plumbea*
Pukeko *Porphyrio porphyrio melanotus*
Banded dotterel *Charadrius bicinctus*
New Zealand shore plover *Thinornis novaeseelandiae*§
Southern great skua *Stercorarius skua lonnbergi*
Southern black-backed gull *Larus dominicanus*
Red-billed gull *L. novaehollandiae scopulinus*
White-fronted tern *Sterna striata*
New Zealand pipit *Anthus novaeseelandiae novaeseelandiae*

Offshore Species

Wandering albatross *Diomedea exulans exulans*
Black-browed mollymawk *D. melanophrys impavida*
Salvin's mollymawk *D. cauta salvini*
Cape pigeon *Daption capense* subsp.
White-headed petrel *Pterodroma lessonii*
Mottled petrel *P. inexpectata*
Flesh-footed shearwater *Puffinus carneipes hullianus*
Buller's shearwater *P. bulleri*
Fluttering shearwater *P. gavia gavia*

Migrants and Vagrants

Rockhopper penguin *Eudyptes chrysocome chrysocome*
Fiordland crested penguin *E. pachyrhynchus*
Erect-crested penguin *E. sclateri*
Grey petrel *Procellaria cinerea*
Black-bellied storm petrel *Fregetta tropica*
Australasian gannet *Sula bassana serrator*
Lesser frigate bird *Fregata ariel ariel*
White heron *Egretta alba modesta*
Reef heron *E. sacra sacra*
Grey teal *Anas gibberifrons gracilis*
South Island pied oystercatcher *Haematopus ostralegus finschi*
Grey plover *Pluvialis squatarola*
Least golden plover *P. fulva*
Asiatic whimbrel *Numenius phaeopus variegatus*
Eastern bar-tailed godwit *Limosa lapponica baueri*
Tattler *Tringa* spp.
Turnstone *Arenaria interpres interpres*
Knot *Calidris canutus canutus*
Arctic skua *Stercorarius parasiticus*
Antarctic tern *Sterna vittata bethunei*
Shining cuckoo *Chrysococcyx lucidus lucidus*
Long-tailed cuckoo *Eudynamys taitensis*

Self-introduced in Historical Times

White-faced heron *Ardea novaehollandiae novaehollandiae*. During 1960s
Mallard *Anas platyrhynchos platyrhynchos*
Spur-winged plover *Vanellus miles novaehollandiae*
Pied stilt *Himantopus himantopus leucocephalus*. First record 1961
Welcome swallow *Hirundo tahitica neoxena*. First seen May 1970
Hedge sparrow *Prunella modularis occidentalis*
Song thrush *Turdus philomelos clarkei*
Blackbird *T. merula merula*
Silvereye *Zosterops lateralis lateralis*. First reported 1856/57
Yellowhammer *Emberiza citrinella caliginosa*. First record 1910
Chaffinch *Fringilla coelebs gengleri*
Greenfinch *Carduelis chloris chloris*. Arrived in 1894
Goldfinch *C. carduelis britannica*
Redpoll *C. flammea cabaret*

Introduced Species

Black swan *Cygnus atratus*. Introduced 1890
California quail *Lophortyx californica brunnescens*
Buff weka *Gallirallus australis hectori*. Introduced 1905
Skylark *Alauda arvensis arvensis*. Introduced prior to 1893
House sparrow *Passer domesticus domesticus*
Starling *Sturnus vulgaris vulgaris*